NUCLEAR WARFARE IN THE MIDDLE EAST: DIMENSIONS AND RESPONSIBILITIES

Leaders, Politics and Social Change
in the Islamic World

Volume 3 in The Kingston Press Series:
Leaders, Politics and Social Change
in the Islamic World

NUCLEAR WARFARE IN THE MIDDLE EAST: DIMENSIONS AND RESPONSIBILITIES

TAYSIR N. NASHIF

The Kingston Press, Inc.
Princeton, N.J. 08542

Copyright © 1984 by The Kingston Press, Inc.
All rights reserved.

No part of this publication may be reproduced, stored in a retrieval system, or transmitted, in any form, by any means, electronic, mechanical, photocopying, recording, or otherwise, without the prior permission of the publisher, except in the case of brief quotations in critical articles or reviews.

Published in the United States of America in 1984
by The Kingston Press, Inc.
  P.O. Box 1456
  Princeton, N.J. 08542

Library of Congress Cataloging in Publication Data

Nashif, Taysir N.
    Nuclear Warfare in the Middle East:
    Dimensions and Responsibilities

    (The Kingston Press series. Leaders, politics,
and social change in the Islamic world: Vol. 3)
    Bibliography: p.
    Includes index.
    1. Atomic weapons. 2. Near East—Armed Forces.
3. Near East—Military policy. I. Title. II. Series.
U264.N37 1984   355'.017'0956   83-25143
ISBN 0-940670-20-8

Views expressed in this book are those of the author and do not necessarily reflect the views of the United Nations.

To Mayyadah, Fawz, Fayruz, and Hanin

Contents

PREFACE	9
INTRODUCTION	11
CHAPTER I: ISRAELI AND ARAB NUCLEAR ACTIVITIES	15
1. Israel Establishes a Nuclear Industry	15
2. Israel's Production of Nuclear Weapons	20
3. Israeli Nuclear Testing	23
4. Arab Nuclear Activities	25
5. Exploration of Nuclear Power in Arab States	30
6. Nuclear Safeguards	32
CHAPTER II: THE RATIONALE FOR ISRAEL'S TAKING A NUCLEAR POSTURE	37
1. Insecurity as a Justification for a Nuclear Option	37
2. Demographic and Economic Factors	40
3. Deterrence	42
4. Changes in the Military Potential of Arab States	46
5. Western Influences on Israeli Attitudes	47
6. Committee for Nuclear Disarmament of the Arab-Israeli Region	49
CHAPTER III: ARAB-ISRAELI NUCLEAR DYNAMICS	53
1. Some Explanations of the Israeli Development of Nuclear Weapons	53
2. Nuclear Policy Alternatives	55
3. Scenarios of Employment of Nuclear Weapons	58
CHAPTER IV: OTHER RISKS LEADING TO NUCLEAR WAR	67
1. Palestinian Guerrilla Organizations and Nuclear Weapons	67
2. Technical Factors Related to the Employment of Nuclear Weapons	68
3. Multiplicity of Nuclear States and Nuclear Weapons: The Middle East as Compared with the United States and the Soviet Union	69
4. Second-Strike Nuclear Balance of Deterrence	72
5. Nuclear Deterrence: Is It Possible?	74

FOURTEEN UNITED NATIONS DOCUMENTS RELATING
TO THE PROLIFERATION OF NUCLEAR DEVICES
IN THE MIDDLE EAST, SOUTH ASIA AND AFRICA 83

SELECTED BIBLIOGRAPHY 133

INDEX 141

PREFACE

In this book I deal with some of the political, military, and psychological implications of the introduction of nuclear weapons into the Middle East, an area of vital importance on the international scene due to the fact that it has been the basis of a continued rivalry among the great powers. Probably there is no topic which needs more to be discussed by governmental officials and in which the public should have a say than the issue of nuclear weapons. The nuclear policy pursued by any state has far-reaching implications not only for the people of that state but also for the peoples of the world.

There is no doubt that this region is facing a grave danger and posing a threat to the rest of the world as well. A number of states there have made or can make nuclear weapons because the means of fabricating fissionable material are readily available. States could attempt to decide military and political problems with nuclear weapons, without understanding the consequences of their use. The modes of thinking of Middle East leaders are still pre-nuclear.

For example, it is difficult for Isreal and the other Middle Eastern countries to calculate precisely the consequences arising from the use of nuclear weapons. In the field of atomic military strategy, there is no possibility to prove the correctness of a school of thought without a test which might end in disaster for both the subject of the experiment and the one conducting it. Many people, of course, predict that there is a high probability that present policies pursued by Middle Eastern states to acquire nuclear weapons will lead to the destruction of the peoples of the area.

Nuclear arms cannot be compared with conventional arms as far as their power is concerned. The use of one nuclear bomb alone would be sufficient to destroy a city with a population of several millions. The explosion would be accompanied by a fire ball surrounded with a ring of thermal radiation and shock waves generating high winds which would spread gamma radioactive dust. For an atomic bomb of average size (say, 20 kilotons), the dust would cover an area measuring 1,000 kilometers in diameter.

A state with nuclear weapons thus has a tremendous advantage in resolving political and military disputes to its own advantage when confronting an adversary which does not possess such weapons. Naturally, it would be tempted to use that power to decide such disputes even though many believe that atomic bombs have made war so devastating that states would not dare to use them. As a matter of fact, the presently existing stockpiles of nuclear weapons, if used, would annihilate the human race and human civilization. Others, however, believe that it would be possible to wage a nuclear war and to escape annihilation. They consider that the consequences of nuclear war might be less horrifying than the consequences of a situation in which there would be no ability or will to fight. They believe it is even possible to win such a war. That is, some strategists have advanced arguments that a thermonuclear total war would be disasterous to everyone, but "small" or "limited" atomic wars would not be. That is, some individuals argue that everything should be done to prevent nuclear war on a large scale, but that such a war could be waged "safely" on a small scale.

The study at hand deals with the nuclear dangers which are facing the Middle East countries and people and which are the result of the interaction of various national, regional and international factors and of various socioeconomic, political and military factors in the Middle East.

A particular debt is owed to Professor Carl Max Kortepeter, of New York University, for the interest, encouragement and intellectual stimulation which he provided to me while writing this book. I am also grateful to Professor Don Peretz, of the State University of New York at Binghamton, to Mr. Robert L. Bull, and to Mr. Douglas M. Rose for their careful reading of the manuscript and their valuable suggestions.

Taysir N.Nashif

INTRODUCTION

The Kingston Press series on Leaders, Politics and Social Change in the Islamic World has been introduced during a particularly difficult period in the history of the Middle East. In the decades following World War I, Turkey and Iran were able to renew their national life in a modern framework leaving behind their imperial pasts. Regrettably, Iran during World War II, under the pretext of wartime necessity, was subjected to the national humiliation of having its leader, Reza Shah, forcibly removed from office and its country occupied by Britain and the Soviet Union.

In the case of the Arabs of the Near East, who had helped the Entente powers of Britain, France and the United States to win World War I by revolting against the Ottoman Turks and their German allies, they simply exchanged the control of the Turks for the mandate and colonial controls of Britain and France. By the time the Arabs gained their independence in the years following World War II, these very same western states, together with the United States, had given the green light for the formation of the new state of Israel. Palestinian refugees resulting from the first Arab-Israeli war in 1948 were settled in the neighboring Arab states of Lebanon, Syria, Jordan and Egypt. These lands were, for the most part, semi-desert societies and only in the second or third year of independent national existence.

To complicate matters further, unlike the interwar years when Turkey and Iran could take a high degree of independent action, the aftermath of World War II produced a weak Europe and a sharp rivalry and polarization between the United States and the Soviet Union. Rivalry between them took the form of a conventional arms race, the stockpiling of nuclear arms, a race for strategic resources, trade embargoes and competition to set up trade, military and ideological blocs.

The West understandably wanted to keep the Arab lands dependent upon its industrial production, but refused to supply them with defensive weapons and aircraft sufficient to protect their homes and states. Meanwhile the Soviet Union had changed from the predominantly agricultural society of Tsarist Russia into an industrial power by the end of World War II. Previously blocked from trade in world markets because of British, French and other trade monopolies, the U.S.S.R. hoped to improve the trade balances of the eastern bloc after World War II when overt colonialism gradually came to an end. In the Mideast disputes arising out of the formation of Israel, the Soviets saw an opportunity to expand trade and to back up their own oil reserves with Mideast oil deals. Arms sales to Egypt in 1955 and subsequently gave to the Soviet bloc a chance to improve Mideast trade and also to become experienced at the West's old games of using such leverage as food diplomacy, trade partnerships, arms sales and military assistance to keep Third World countries friendly.

Clearly then, three events had greatly heightened the tensions in the Middle East after World War II: the formation of the state of Israel; the determination of some Arab states, notably Egypt under Nasser and Syria since 1954, to become independent of European manipulation and control; and the ability of the Soviet Union, since the mid-sixties, to protect its own interests.

With the assistance of some western powers and the U.S.S.R., Egypt and Syria demonstrated clearly in the Yom Kippur/Ramadan war of 1973 that Arabs could make a studied technological leap, thus shaking Israel's previous monopoly of advanced military technology. This development became possible only with the shift of billions of petro-dollars into the Middle East economy.

These are the shifts in Middle Eastern politics and economics that have given rise to the specter of nuclear proliferation in the Middle East, the issues of which are discussed by Dr. Nashif.

Already in the 1950's the western powers aided Israel in the building of nuclear reactors for peaceful pursuits and instructed her scientists in the latest developments in atomic physics. Exchange visits of Jewish and other scientists to Israel and the West also facilitated the flow of advanced technology to Israel. With the acquisition of nuclear reactors, heavy water plants and ample supplies of fissionable materials, it was no big scientific leap for Israel to produce atomic weapons with budgets beefed up by the United States. With the placing of atomic research (and presumably bomb production) within its own vast defense establishment, Israel could claim immunity from international inspection either from the United Nations or the United States Atomic Energy Commission. These are but some of the issues Dr. Nashif discusses in his description of Israel's acquisition of nuclear weapons.

Introduction 13

Israel's rationale is quite clear: Arab technical skills and the number of trained Arab military personnel have reached the point where, without the leverage of some new technology, the Arab states are, or soon will be, in a position to challenge Israel's conventional military superiority. Moreover, world leaders have become more sophisticated about Arab interests and rights; thus, Israel, not unlike the United States vis-à-vis the U.S.S.R., has come to rely on the threat of nuclear weapons to keep the Arabs from defending rights which they consider legitimate.

But Dr. Nashif has carried the analysis further. How can any state, he muses, believe that it can maintain indefinitely a monopoly of nuclear weaponry? Israel's "going nuclear" actually appears to invite nuclear proliferation in southwest Asia.

Arabs, like the Jews, have a history of persecution and political weakness, which heightens their feelings of mutual distrust. The current policy of feeding factionalism and inviting U.S. gunboats, aircraft and Marines into the Middle East to underwrite Israeli objectives only obscures basic issues even more. By resorting to the crude gunboat diplomacy of the nineteenth century, the United States risks reaping a whirlwind into which vital American political and economic interests could be swept.

By contrast to these stark possibilities, the fourteen United Nations documents appended to this essay offer to the reader a ray of idealism and hope. They present a number of attempts by the United Nations to have the Middle East and other areas declared nuclear-free zones. This position is in sharp contrast to the new round of nuclear proliferation of the U.S. and the Soviet Union. Dr. Nashif rightly questions whether Israel or any Middle Eastern state can afford to install the sophisticated "fail-safe" devices and then play the nuclear games of the U.S. and the U.S.S.R.

With this brief review of the background of Middle Eastern events leading directly to the present impasse, I welcome Dr. Nashif to the series and our readers to an important discussion of the consequences of nuclear proliferation in the Middle East.

C. Max Kortepeter
New York University

Chapter I

Israeli and Arab Nuclear Activities

1. Israel Establishes a Nuclear Industry

Israel's nuclear research began before the end of the 1948-49 Palestine War. Chaim Weizmann, the first President of Israel, was a specialist in organic chemistry and had links with renowned nuclear scientists in the West. He was well aware of the importance of creating a facility for nuclear energy in Israel. Before and after the declaration of the state of Israel (May 14, 1948), Jewish nuclear scientists immigrated to the Jewish state. In 1949, a number of students were sent to Western countries to specialize in nuclear sciences. Finally, nuclear research was begun in at least three institutions of higher learning in Israel: The Hebrew University of Jerusalem, the Weizmann Institute at Rehovot and the Technion at Haifa.

In 1949, a Department of Isotope Research was established at the Weizmann Institute and in 1953, when Israeli students began returning from the West, this department was enlarged and converted into the Department of Nuclear Physics. Dr. Israel Dostrowsky, a staff member of this department, developed a process for the production of heavy water, necessary for the operation of reactors, by a chemical method which did not require electrical energy.

A scientific unit affiliated with the Department of Research and Planning of the Ministry of Defense was established. The Israeli Atomic Energy Commission (AEC) was set up in June 1952, but its existence was publicly revealed only in 1954. Throughout the 1950s, the AEC, chaired by Professor Ernst David Bergmann, was under the control of the Ministry of Defense, which was committed, according to Simha Flapan, an Israeli writer, to the production of an atomic bomb.[1]

The AEC was given its own budget and laboratories. The AEC was organized within the Ministry of Defense and, as a result, technical assistance could be obtained from the Israeli armed forces. Strict secrecy concerning the nuclear program could be assured more readily than it would be if a public organization had been given responsibility.[2] The AEC submitted a proposal for the construction of a 600-megawatt nuclear reactor and the government of Israel approved the project.[3] A number of Western states agreed to help Israel financially and scientifically to build reactors, for example, by offering to train the technicians that were needed to operate reactors.[4] As a result, Israel now has the capacity to produce electricity from nuclear power and to make the plutonium used in nuclear devices as well, from the nuclear facilities it built at Dimona, Nahal Soreq and elsewhere in the country.[5] Experts have observed that Israeli scientists could build a chemical separation plant for processing plutonium into weapon-grade material.[6] Also, by 1953, Israel developed the capability to produce heavy water and enriched uranium. This was made possible after Israel signed an agreement with France according to which France bought Israel Dostrowsky's patents for the production of heavy water and for the preparation of low-grade uranium from phosphate. In return, France opened its nuclear institutions to Israeli scientists who received their training there.[7] Then, in 1955, Israel obtained a nuclear reactor from the United States with a five-megawatt capacity, established in Neve Rubin, to train scientists and technicians in the field of nuclear research and development.[8] Under the same agreement, Israel obtained from the United States a large scientific library that included 6,500 reports on United States nuclear research, and the opportunity to train Israelis at United States nuclear installations. Later on, another nuclear reactor was bought from the United States and constructed at the Technion, which had a capacity of eight-megawatts, to train doctoral students in nuclear physics and nuclear chemistry.[9]

In 1957, David Ben Gurion, then Prime Minister and Minister of Defense, proposed to the Israeli Cabinet the construction of a nuclear reactor at Dimona. This was agreed to and a reactor, with a capacity of 24 megawatts, was supplied by France. It uses natural uranium and is moderated by heavy water. According to W. B. Bader, it can produce sufficient fissionable material for about one small atomic bomb annually.[10] It appears to Palit and Namboodiri that the decision in 1957 to construct the reactor was taken just after the Israelis had made the decision to make nuclear weapons.[11] In 1958, a reactor from the United States was constructed at Rishon Letzion with a capacity of five megawatts.

By the early 1960s, the reactor at Dimona began to attract outside attention although Israel has never allowed international inspection or control, arguing that the reactor is located inside a military zone.[12] Palit and Namboodiri point out, as well, that Israel also claimed that outside inspection was not necessary because adequate measures had been taken to assure the safe operation of the reactor. This means that Israel has complete control over the plutonium which the reactor produces.[13] The reactor can produce 24 grams of plutonium 239 per day. Thus, annual plutonium production is slightly over eight kilograms.[14] To manufacture a nuclear device with the lethal capacity of the Hiroshima bomb, about five kilograms of weapon-grade plutonium are needed.[15] If we assume for the sake of argument that the reactor began production at its full capacity in 1965 (some say that production started in 1962 and others say the end of 1964), by the end of 1974 it sould have produced about 81 kilograms of plutonium 239. This amount is sufficient for the manufacture of about eight atomic bombs of the type dropped on Nagasaki in 1945, which required about 10,441 grams.[16] If the reactor was producing only weapons-grade plutonium, one may estimate that Israel by 1977 had accumulated fissionable material sufficient to manufacture some 15 to 20 nuclear weapons in the kiloton range.[17]

The government of Israel at first would not admit that it had constructed a reactor at Dimona. This large installation was claimed to be a textile factory. The reactor's existence was acknowledged in 1960: It is not easy to conceal a nuclear reactor of 24 megawatts for a long time. David Ben Gurion, then Israel's Prime Minister, announced that the reactor was for "peaceful needs." Avraham Herman, Israel's former ambassador to the United States, indicated that the reactor was designed to produce electricity. Other Israeli governmental representatives claimed that its purpose was for "research needs." These explanations were received by politicians, technicians and scientists skeptically. They asked why a small state like Israel would be willing to invest such a vast sum (hundreds of millions of Israeli pounds) on a reactor for research purposes. And, what state has ever built a reactor for the production of electricity in the desert, far from the sea or from water sources? And if the reactor really was dedicated to nonmilitary purposes, why then was it not open and subject to a civil developmental authority, as is the case in all the states possessing reactors of this sort? And, why was the plant under the exclusive supervision of the Ministry of Defense, and why had much time passed before even the parliament (Knesset) knew about it? Many people became disturbed when the existence of the Dimona installation was discovered. The cause of this reaction was the secrecy surrounding the reactor's construction. But more importantly, this reaction arose after people came to understand the implication that nuclear weapons could be made by Israel and would be introduced into the Middle East. For one, as W. B. Bader has pointed out, the President of the United States, J. F. Kennedy, was disturbed; he placed heavy pressure on David Ben Gurion to bring the Dimona facility under international supervision.[18] Ben Gurion refused to allow such inspections. Some newspapers speculated, however, that the United States actually did reach an agreement with Israel according to which engineers from the U.S. Atomic Energy Commission would be allowed to carry out informal, unpublished annual inspections. If such an arrangement actually had been worked out, it would have benefitted Israel by reassuring the United States that Israel was not manufacturing atomic weapons and, at the same time, keeping Arab states in a state of uncertainty regarding whether or not Israel was pursuing a nuclear option for its military.

By contrast to the Dimona facility, the reactor at Nahal Soreq has never aroused any doubt regarding its military nuclear purpose.[19] In the mid-1960s, Israel was offered a desalination plant by the United States. United States officials maintained that through this plant, Israel would derive economic benefits and it would be possible for the United States to allay the suspicion and distrust enveloping Israel's nuclear activities and to set up an international inspection system for all nuclear facilities in the Middle East.[20] The condition that the United States had attached to constructing the plant was that Israel accept international inspection of the Dimona reactor. Israel turned down the United States offer because of this condition, even though the plant was of potential economic benefit to Israel. This refusal indicated rather clearly what the Israelis have been seeking to achieve through their atomic energy facility at Dimona.[21]

In the end, in return for providing Israel with generous supplies of conventional arms, the United States administration finally did win the right to inspect the Dimona reactor. Although United States scientists periodically visited Dimona to make sure that no plutonium separation plant was built, as United States officials stated, these visits were inadequate guarantees that the reactor would be used solely for peaceful purposes.[22] Then, in November 1976, a delegation of United States senators touring the Middle East to survey the potential of countires in the Middle East to produce nuclear weapons was prevented from seeing the Israeli research reactor at Dimona.[23]

Some argue that if Israel had set up a plutonium separation plant, it would have been apparent because such plants are very difficult to conceal.[24] This factor might have played a role in the Israelis' announced decision not to build such a plant. Palit and Namboodiri, however, claim that a number of separation or reprocessing facilities to produce weapons-grade plutonium actually were built in "hot laboratories" near the two nuclear reactors at Dimona and Nahal Soreq.[25] In addition, on May 5, 1969, *Der Spiegel* published a report that Israel had established a plant for plutonium separation near Dimona, under the supervision of Dr. Ernst David Bergmann, buying the equipment piece by piece in order not to raise the suspicions of a number of Western countries.[26] Then, it was reported that two nuclear scientists from Israel received the rights from France and West Germany to produce enriched uranium by using lasers.[27] This technology, of course, could provide weapons-grade material.[28] Chari has pointed out that supplies of fissionable material for reactors were met by Israel through shipments of hundreds of tons of natural uranium from various countries such as Argentina, France, Canada, Great Britain, and West Germany.[29] It also was discovered that the Scientific Unit of the Israeli Ministry of Defense carried out studies which revealed the existence of uranium in the phosphate of the Negev. The total uranium available in these deposits of phosphate ores is estimated to be 25,000 tons.[30] Bader also noted that Israel has developed the capability of producing heavy water and of deriving uranium as a by-product of the phosphate fertilizer industry. It is quite probable that Israel is using this uranium to fuel the Dimona reactor and to produce weapon-grade plutonium.

2. Israel's Production of Nuclear Weapons

Many nuclear scientists believe that Israel has designed and manufactured nuclear weapons, in view of the availability to Israel of sufficient technical information and of nuclear scientists, together with the cooperation of Jewish scientists from the West.[32] In addition, since 1970, reports have regularly been published indicating that Israel has moved into a new stage of nuclear policy and nuclear-weapon development. Many specialists assume that Israel can fabricate a nuclear bomb quickly.[33] Indeed some Israeli officials have claimed that Israel has the capability to manufacture nuclear weapons in a relatively short time if necessary. Such a necessity might emerge, in the view of Katzir, former president of Israel, "in the light of changes that occur in the policies of each of Egypt, Syria, Jordan and the Soviet Union in the future."[34]

W. B. Bader agrees that "there is no doubt that Israel has the technological capacity to develop a modest nuclear striking force without significant outside help."[35] And, Edward Teller, the U.S. atomic scientist, who is known as the father of the hydrogen bomb, announced on December 12, 1965, following his visit to Israel, that nothing prevents Israel from manufacturing atomic bombs inasmuch as it has all that it needs for this purpose, including experts, equipment, or plutonium.[36]

In 1968, the United States Central Intelligence Agency (CIA) determined that fissionable materials were missing from the United States and probably shipped to Israel. The report concluded that Israel was soon to become a nuclear power. Former CIA Director, Richard Helms, in his testimony before the United States Senate Foreign Relations Committee on July 7, 1970, stated that Israel can produce modern arms.

In 1968, the United States Central Intelligence Agency reported that Israel already possessed atomic weapons. This report was secret until Carl Duckett, the CIA's Deputy Director for Science and Technology from 1967 to 1977, informed the United States Nuclear Regulatory Commission about its contents in February of 1976. This information was included in an unclassified report in 1978. Duckett told the Commission that the CIA had varied evidence to support its 1968 report. This evidence consisted of the special type of bombing practice which Israel's A-4 jets went through and which only fits the purpose of delivering nuclear weapons. Through the employment of highly sophisticated "sniffers" to monitor soil and air samples from around Dimona nuclear facility, the CIA obtained evidence that Israel had enough highly enriched uranium to manufacture a number of bombs.[37] The CIA expressed its belief in another report, dated September 1974, that Israel already has produced nuclear weapons; "Our judgement is based on Israeli acquisition of uranium, partly by clandestine means; the ambiguous nature of Israeli efforts in the field of uranium enrichment; and Israel's large investment in a costly missile system designed to accommodate nuclear warheads."[38] The summary of the 1974 report was released in 1978 by the CIA under the Freedom of Information Act to the National Resources Defense Council. By 1976, the CIA researchers came to the conclusion that the Israelis were extracting plutonium from the Dimona facility. Again, Duckett revealed, in early 1976, that Israel "has ten to twenty nuclear weapons ready and available for use."[39]

A. Haselkorn, an Israeli political scientist, maintains that if Israel had decided to build nuclear weapons, the critical judgment was taken in the middle of 1970. Haselkorn is of the view that an Israeli "worst-case-planning" approach, "*must* assume that Moscow *knew* . . . the truth (or "almost" the truth) about the real state of the Israeli nuclear option." In mid-1970 the Soviet Union became involved in the defense of Egypt, which brought about an alteration of the political and strategic environment of Israel. Haselkorn maintains that against such a background it was almost inevitable that Israel would decide to manufacure nuclear weapons.[40] The development of nuclear weapons would give a greater sense of security to Israel. The Israelis felt that a state with nuclear weapons could behave with less indecision when under the threat of attack. Thus, Haselkorn maintains that the decision, probably taken in 1970, to choose the nuclear option, was prompted solely by short-range considerations. That is, the Soviet military presence in Egypt (before the Soviet advisers were driven out of the country) led Israel to take the view that possession of a secret nuclear bomb was strategically desirable.[41]

Others agree that Israel has some type of nuclear weapons capability. The *SIPRI Yearbook 1972*, for example, stated that several private reports, some apparently emanating from United States intelligence, indicated that Israel does indeed have a crude nuclear weapons capability.[42]

Palit and Namboodiri claimed that by 1973 it was beyond doubt that Israel had developed nuclear weapons.[43] Andre Beaufre, of the French Institute for Strategic Studies, said to Muhammad Hasanein Heykal on November 24, 1973 that he believed that

Israel has a possiblity of manufacturing atomic weapons, and if its government were to take a political decision to manufacture such bombs, then these bombs could be ready in a matter of six months; I do not exclude at all that in some place in Israel there is a number of atomic bombs, though I would imagine that these bombs, if existing, are primitive types made when the bomb was in its infancy... namely 'fat' bombs in their size and limited in their power.[44]

The Times of London wrote on December 3, 1974 that the production of fissionable material in Israel enabled it to have made a total of six or seven bombs. It was reported that Israel could manufacture one atomic bomb every year.[45].

At a conference on proliferation in 1974 a poll was taken on the probability that one or more Arab states and Israel would acquire nuclear weapons. Twenty out of 25 students of nuclear proliferation expressed the opinion that Israel either already possessed a nuclear weapon or would have one before 1978. Nearly as many thought that at least one Arab state would possess nuclear weapons within a decade.

In testimony before the United States Congress in November 1975, William Colby, former director of the United States CIA, testified that Israel had secretly diverted fissionable material and was well on its way to manufacturing a nuclear bomb.[47] A report dated March 1976 revealed that CIA officials were of the opinion that Israel possessed 10 to 20 nuclear bombs "ready and available for use."[48]

Wehrtechnik, the semiofficial West German army monthly, wrote in June 1976 that Levi Eshkol, who succeeded Ben Gurion as prime minister, discovered in 1963 that Defense Minister Moshe Dayan at the time had ordered the assembly of nuclear bombs secretly. *Wehrtechnik* further revealed that, according to Western reports, by 1963 Israel had staged an underground test in the Negev and that soon afterwards preparations for the assembly of an atom bomb had started. In 1969, according to the West German journal, the tests were successfully completed but production of the bomb was not begun because Israeli scientists wanted to cut production time.

Finally, the United States magazine *Newsweek* wrote on September 12, 1977, "Some United States intelligence analysis concluded that the bomb the South Africans had planned to set off actually had been made in Israel."

Reports reveal that Israeli governmental officials conducted negotiations as early as December, 1968 with the United Sates administration to acquire Phantom jets equipped with bomb racks adapted for carrying nuclear weapons.[49] Also, Israel has received from the United States Lance surface-to-surface missiles which are capable of carrying conventional and nuclear weapons.

The New York Times, in an article on Israeli military power, reported that Israel had developed the Jericho missile, which is reportedly capable of carrying a 1,000-1,500 pound warhead, and quoted United States intelligence sources as saying that the only rationale for such missiles is that they are capable of delivering a nuclear warhead.[50] *Jane's All the World Aircraft* for the years 1970-71, 1971-72 and 1972-73 contained similar reports[51] and William Beecher, the military affairs editor of *The New York Times*, quoted a source as saying that "it wouldn't make much sense to manufacture a costly weapon like the Jericho merely to carry the equivalent of two or three 500-pound bombs. The decision to go into production strongly suggests Israel has, or believes it could soon have, nuclear warheads for the system."[52] Beecher further observed that analysts maintain "Israel may have a number of nuclear-weapon components that could be assembled quickly, in a crisis, for use on the Jericho as well as on jet fighter-bombers."[53]

Israel's former Foreign Minister, Abba Eban, was often asked about the speculation that his country possessed atomic weapons. He did not refute them and replied that he was not competent to discuss technical details of armaments, but emphasized Israel's long-standing policy of refusing to be the first to introduce nuclear weapons into the Middle East.[54]

3. Israeli Nuclear Testing

Related to the question of Israel's capability of developing nuclear weapons is the question of nuclear testing. William B. Bader claimed that, because of Israel's imited borders before the June

1967 War, "an atmospheric test was clearly out of the question... and underground testing... would have been dangerous if venting occurred."[55] However, it is questionable that Israel would set up a nuclear arsenal with untested bombs and further put its trust in such bombs.[56] To the contrary, some experts are of the view that there is no necessity to test a nuclear device as long as its design and assembly are accomplished according to the methods for producing atomic devices that have previously been established. In *Nuclear Threat in the Middle East,* Pranger and Tahtinen pointed out that no first nuclear test has ever failed.[57] A state could rely, if not completely, then at least considerably, on the possible performance of its weapons on theoretical grounds, namely, without having to test them. In *Nuclear Theft: Risks and Safeguards,* Willrich and Taylor noted that the type of bomb dropped on Hiroshima had never been tested.[58] Clearly, however, if a nuclear weapon need not to be tested, the triggering device should be.[59]

Israel probably has made an underground test of a nuclear device in the Sinai or in the Al-Naqab (the Negev). In one of the United States underground nuclear tests, on December 3, 1966, an atomic bomb was exploded at a depth of 1100 meters without the test being discovered. This feat was accomplished by suspending the bomb in an area, surrounded by air, which served as a cushion, which absorbed the main shocks caused by the explosion. It is also possible to conduct such a test nearer to the surface of the earth, provided the underground gap is wider.

It is not inconceivable that Israel obtained the results of nuclear tests conducted by France when the two states were cooperating in the development of nuclear weapons in the 1960s. Heikal stated that Israel could, as a result, prepare for an atomic test.[61]

Some reports strongly indicate that Israel has conducted an underground nuclear test in Al-Naqab (the Negev), at a depth of 800 meters, at about the end of September or the beginning of October 1966.[62] The reports are supported by the fact that a short while before, a group of 11 Israeli nuclear engineers were sent to the United States to be trained on the technology of underground nuclear explosions. Upon their return, according to 'Azmi, they immediately started work in Al-Naqab (the Negev) to construct a site for such tests.[63]

That Israel may have conducted tests also was indicated when an American scientist working on a marine research vessel to determine the amount of tritium in Mediterranean waters during September and October 1966 noticed that the percentage of radioactive concentration in these waters had risen. The same fact was noted by three other scientists from the United States and West Germany, who were engaged in similar research in the Gulf of 'Aqabah. These scientists attributed this phenomenon to the possibility that there had been an underground nuclear explosion which would have produced a rise in the level of radioactivity in deep sea water. Some argue that because of the extremely harmful effects of nuclear explosions, Israel decided not to conduct nuclear tests above ground.[64] Also the element of surprise would be lost and the violation of international agreements would be clear.

On 22 September 1979, a United States VELA satellite over the South African coast, a United States observatory at Arecibo in Puerto Rico and the United States Naval Research Laboratory registered signs near Prince Edward Islands off the South African coast. The Naval Research Laboratory and United States intelligence sources were convinced that these were the signs of a nuclear explosion. Rumors circulated that the South Africans and Israelis were involved in this. In February 1980, about five months after the mysterious event, Dan Raviv, an Israeli-American CBS Radio correspondent in Tel Aviv filed from Rome a report that "CBS News has learned that Israel exploded a nuclear bomb last September, in the Atlantic Ocean off the coast of South Africa. Informed sources [in Israel] confirm that this was an Israeli nuclear test—conducted with the help and cooperation of the South African government."[65] Even as early as 1961 Gottleib noted that the Israeli military research establishment had a number of large laboratories and had technicians who know how to detonate nuclear devices.[66]

4. Arab Nuclear Activities

Arabs think that Israel has developed a nuclear capability. Their military appraisals must take this into consideration, for the Arab confrontation states (probably excluding, at present, Egypt) of course feel threatened. Others note that the initial reaction of Arab states to Israel's great interest in or the acquisition of nuclear weapons has ranged from "feigned nonchalance to defiance to attempts towards developing nuclear capability themselves."[67] Bell, however, has noted that among Arabs, "there has... been a deep reluctance to examine the implications of [an Israeli nuclear weapon... and in] conventional Arab war plans a minimum of space seems to be given to the nuclear dimension."[68] Whoever is correct, many have observed a marked change in Arab attitudes toward Israel's nuclear program. We have an indication of the Arab concern over Israel's acquisition of nuclear capability by noting the response of the former Egyptian President, Jamal 'Abd al-Nasir, to rumors circulated in 1960 that Israel was developing nuclear weapons. 'Abd al-Nasir stated that if it were true that Israel was trying to build a nuclear device, it would mean the beginning of war between Egypt and Israel because Egypt could not permit Israel to succeed in manufacturing an atomic bomb.

A number of Arab states in consequence of Israel's nuclear activities have also embarked on nuclear research even though Arab states do not possess sufficient trained manpower or industrial infrastructure to implement a nuclear-weapons program. Livneh, however, maintained that they can undertake to develop a militarily significant nuclear program.[69] Some Arab states, in fact, are training their first generation of nuclear scientists and technical experts. They also are using oil, petrodollars and favorable international conditions. The Economic Research Institute for the Middle East, a research organization based in Tokyo, stated that in April, 1976 there were 15 nuclear reactors planned or contracted for the Middle East.[70] Egypt, for one, has been showing an interest in conducting nuclear research and development. Even though Egypt's ability, in technical terms, to produce nuclear weapons domestically was considered to be doubtful, it still could acquire nuclear weapons by relying on foreign technical assistance. Thus, Palit and Namboodiri, for example, maintain that the first credible Arab attempt to begin a strategic nuclear dialogue with Israel was made by Egypt.[71] This attempt was credible because Egypt was a confrontation state and it already owned a delivery system that could reach Israeli targets.

In September 1955 it was learned that the Egyptian Government had made financial allocations for atomic research and development.[72] Since 1955, Egypt has fostered some activity in the field of nuclear-energy research and uses of nuclear energy with assistance from states in both the Eastern and Western blocs. Its first atomic research two-megawatt reactor was supplied by the Soviet Union and constructed and operated by Soviet experts at Anshas in northeastern Egypt. Egyptian technicians were trained in 1956 to operate reactors producing electricity. The Soviet-supplied reactor was started up in 1961 with enriched uranium from the Soviet Union. The reactor was too small to produce any significant amount of plutonium for a military purpose.[73]

The Soviet reactor was visited by experts of the International Atomic Energy Agency (IAEA).[74] It was also inspected by United States experts who approved of its design.[75] The IAEA established the Afro-Asian Center for Radio-Isotope Research near this reactor. The center, which is under international supervision, conducts research on medical, agricultural, and industrial questions.

Egypt also made agreements with India and Yugoslavia which the IAEA encouraged. In March 1961, the Egyption daily, *Al-Ahram*, reported talks between Egyptian and Yugoslav scientists conducted to seek ways to develop nuclear energy. Also, the *New York Tribune* reported on February 16, 1961 that a number of scientists, mostly from West Germany, were invited to Egypt to work on a plan for atomic development. The Egyptian newspaper *Akhbar al-Yawm* further reported that earlier, on February 12, 1961, a delegation of scientists from West Germany had come to Egypt as early as January 21, 1961 and that an agreement had been signed in Bonn between Egypt and the Federal Republic of Germany for the construction of a nuclear reactor for the production of electricity. The fuel for the operation of the reactor was to be natural uranium and heavy water would be used as the moderator.[76]

According to the Israeli daily *Ma'ariv* of August 23, 1962, there were in Egypt in 1962, 12 British atomic scientists, 13 Czechs and 21 Japanese. At the same time, Egyptian researchers worked in the Soviet Union, the United States, Britain, West Germany, India, Norway, and Austria. In early 1963, it was decided that a reactor, with a capacity of 100-120 megawatts, would be constructed to the west of Alexandria. The Israeli daily *Davar* reported on April 30, 1963 that Soviet experts would perform the major part of the construction for the reactor. Kennedy and Dunkin, a British firm, was invited to offer consultancy services and planning with respect to the reactor, and in April a contract was signed with that firm.[77]

An important component of the atomic industry is the production of heavy water. In response to a request by the Egyptian Government, an expert was sent by the IAEA to make an appraisal of the merits of establishing a project in Egypt. V. Thayer, from the Atomic Energy Department of Du Pont, who was sent by the IAEA, disapproved, in his report, of the plan on economic and not technical grounds. In his view, there is in the United States a surplus of heavy water and therefore it would not be wise to establish such a project. It is of relevance to mention here that the company with which he was affiliated is one of the largest producers of plutonium and heavy water in the world, although Egypt did not accept its recommendation. A project for producing a heavy water facility was set up by the German company Hoechst Farben Werke.[78]

Some Israelis viewed the Egyptian efforts to develop nuclear reactors as an attempt to produce nuclear weapons in the future.

In September 1973, the IAEA published the results of a survey on the requirements for nuclear power stations in 14 developing countries: Greece, Turkey, Yugoslavia, Egypt, Pakistan, Bangladesh, Thailand, the Philippines, Singapore, Korea, Argentina, Chile, Jamaica, and Mexico. The Egyptian Government forecast the need for a nuclear power reactor with a capacity of 400 megawatts in 1980, and another reactor of the same capacity in 1982. (The two reactors on which former President Gerald Ford and the late President Anwar al-Sadat had agreed in Washington, D.C., in November 1975 have, it seems, a capacity of 600 megawatts each.) In 1974, the United States and the Soviet Union promised to supply Egypt with nuclear power stations. In June 1974, President Nixon signed, when on a visit to Cairo, an agreement with Al-Sadat to supply a nuclear power station, and in November 1974, the Soviet Union agreed to provide Egypt with additional power reactors. In January 1975, Egyptian-French discussions were conducted on providing Egypt with two nuclear power stations and nuclear technology, perhaps with Iranian or Saudi financing. In November 1975, Al-Sadat reached an agreement to purchase two American nuclear power reactors. For over a year, a United States nuclear engineering consulting company worked in Egypt conducting surveys within the framework of the Egyptian nuclear program.[79]

Egypt also developed strong ties with India, which conducted a nuclear explosion in May 1974, and with Pakistan, which is engaged in the establishment of the main components of a nuclear industry.[80]

In 1975, an engineering feasibility survey was carried out on the use of nuclear explosives to excavate a 70-kilometer canal from the Mediterranean to the Qattarah Depression. An artificial lake also was to be created and filled with water up to 70 meters deep from which Egypt might generate nearly 10,000 megawatts of electricity. This survey was conducted by a West German engineering consulting firm and it lasted about 18 months. Then Egypt turned to the United States and the Sovient Union for technical assistance to dig the projected canal. The Egyptian Minister of Electric Power indicated that the reaction of the two superpowers was quite encouraging.[81] Spokesmen of the State Department confirmed that the United States would agree to provide limited technical assistance to Egypt. They claimed that the subject of supplying Egypt with nuclear explosive materials for this purpose had not reached the stage of a formal Egyptian request.[82]

With the assistance of the United States and some European states, Egypt made attempts to establish a pan-Arab association devoted to the study of nuclear sciences probably in an effort to assert its leadership in nuclear sciences in the Arab world.

During the Ford Administration (mid-1970s) the Egyptian Minister for Electric Power stated that the Egyptians wanted to purchase nuclear power stations from the United States, West Germany, and France. The first station, as agreed with former President Ford, would be American. Afterwards, nuclear stations would be ordered from France and, later on, from West Germany.

Egypt plans to buy power reactors for the production of electricity; it wishes to develop the capacity to use nuclear energy for civil purposes, including the desalination of water. Of course, it also wants to develop the capability to produce uranium and thorium.

According to the plan drawn up by the international and Egyptian teams, eight power reactors, each with a capacity of 600 megawatts, would go into operation in Egypt during the period 1980-1990 and they would have a total nuclear power capacity of 4800 megawatts.[83]

5. Exploration of Nuclear Power in Arab States

Egypt made surveys (between 1956 and 1960) on the availability of uranium in its territory. These surveys indictaed there were uranium deposits in the eastern and western deserts, in the heavy mineral sands of the Nile delta, the shores of the Mediterranean, and in phosphate rocks throughout the country. Extensive deposits of uranium oxide and thorium oxide were found in the heavy mineral sands; according to one estimate, there are about 370,000 tons of thorium oxide and 28,000 tons of uranium oxide,[84] which could be recovered as a by-product of the exploitation of the sands for other minerals. It would theoretically be possible to produce 40 to 50 tons of uranium oxide and about 600 tons of thorium oxide per annum as a million tons of minerals were recovered.[85] Also, it is estimated that the quantities of uranium oxide in phosphate rocks in Eqypt amount to 100,000 tons, but given the present state of technical knowledge, of the known phosphates deposits only about half of them could be mined.[86]

Egypt has not been the only Arab state which is interested in the nuclear field. Colonel Mu'ammar Al-Qadhdhafi of Libya reportedly made attempts to purchase nuclear devices. However, probably due to the simplistic nature of such attempts, it would be a gross exaggeration to argue, as some do, that they were to be used to start a nuclear confrontation with Israel. One might say that even if he were successful in buying nuclear devices, a nuclear threat to Israel would not necessarily meet with success for Libya; it involves more than the purchase of nuclear devices to conduct an effective nuclear confrontation.

Iraq also has made some strides in the nuclear field that might have led to its acquisition of a nuclear capability. A nuclear reactor in Iraq to the south of Baghdad was supplied by the Soviet Union. Yet the reactor, which started operation in 1968, is too small to produce any significant amount of plutonium for military purposes.[87] In 1975, France agreed to build a nuclear reactor for Iraq, but in early 1979 it was blown up in Toulon by saboteurs just before it was to have been shipped to Iraq. The newspaper *Action* reported on June 23, 1980 that "a replacement has been under construction and is scheduled to go into operation sometime next year."[88]

The French followed through on their promise. However, Yahya al-Mashhad, an Egyptian and a former Cairo University professor who was working for the Iraqi Atomic Energy Commission, and had been at the Center for Nuclear Studies at Fontenay-aux-Rose, France, was found murdered in June 1980. This, of course, set the plans of the Iraqis back even further. Nevertheless, citing governmental sources in Washington, D.C., *The New York Times* reported on March 18, 1980 that Italy supplied Iraq with necessary equipment which could be used in the production of plutonium. Next the French weekly *Vendredi, Samedi, Dimanche* reported on April 3, 1980 that Iraq and India had signed a nuclear cooperation agreement which enabled Iraq to receive technical knowledge from Indian scientists who worked in the Indian nuclear program. The Hebrew daily *Haaretz* reported on July 17, 1980 that France once again had provided Iraq with a large nuclear reactor and assisted it with training nuclear scientists. France also provided Iraq with enriched uranium. Finally, Pakistan has been engaged in nuclear activities and some Arab states, notably Libya and Saudi Arabia, have assisted it financially.

Bombings and threats have been directed against the Pakistani nuclear program and against European firms which sell nuclear equipment to Pakistan. For example, on February 20, 1981, a bomb exploded at the home of the managing director of CORA Engineering, a Swiss company that was building, according to Weissman and Krosney, "key components for the Pakistani enrichment plant at Kahuta."[89] It has been revealed that this company signed a contract to supply Pakistan with a second gasification and solidification plant, which is an essential part in the centrifuge process. The group responsible for the bombing was not identified. As one possible result, Alcom, an Italian company, under a contract to build reprocessing vessels for the Pakistanis cancelled the contract.

It was also reported in Weissman and Krosney that a small family firm, called Hans Waelischmiller, in the German city of Markdorf, had sold the Pakistanis, sometime in the late 1970s, some special lead shielding for protection against radiation, special remote-controlled equipment to move radioactive substances, manipulators and transporters of sensitive nuclear materials, all essential equipment for nuclear facilities at the New Labs near Islamabad and the Chashma Reprocessing Plant.[90] This German firm was also a target for explosives and threatening telephone calls by an unidentified group.

6. Nuclear Safeguards

Before concluding this chapter, we shall consider briefly the effectiveness of safeguards in preventing diversion of nuclear technology to military use and also Israel's attitude to the Non-Proliferation Treaty (NPT), which has been supported by the overwhelming majority of the members of the United Nations, including the Soviet Union and the United States. The by-products of fission in nuclear power plants are the basic material used in the fission bomb. As increasing amounts of weapon-grade plutonium 239 are being produced by the nuclear power industry, states or even nonstate organizations have a greater opportunity to use nuclear materials to develop nuclear weapons. With respect to the ease with which states and organizations can secure large amounts of plutonium or uranium, Mason Willrich and Theodore Taylor state that nuclear safeguards are so inadequate that interested groups may easily be able to remove essential fissionable materials from nuclear power plants.[91] The prevention of fissionable materials from being accumulated or acquired by various states and by interested organizations is not global in scope, nor is it effective. Also, according to *The Defense Monitor*, a publication of the Center for Defense Information in Washington, D.C., "U.S. Army Special Forces exercises have shown that nuclear weapons storage areas can be penetrated successfully without detection despite guards, fences, and sensors. Their example could obviously be followed by a daring and well-organized ... organization."[92]

Nuclear physicist Ralph Lapp maintains that a dedicated group of skilled scientists and technicians in the field of bomb making might fashion "a modestly effective implosion bomb."[93] Such a group also could use it's plutonium in a technically simpler radiation dispersal device; it is possible to transform the plutonium into an aerosol of finely divided particles that could be distributed uniformly into the intake of a large office building's air-conditioning system. According to Willrich and Taylor, only 3.5 ounces of this extremely toxic substance would create a deadly hazard to everyone in the building.[94]

States which drafted the Non-Proliferation Treaty had the developments described above in mind when they drafted this treaty. A state's signature on the NPT means that it will not develop or possess nuclear arms and that it will place all nuclear facilities in their lands under international control in return for a commitment by the Super Powers that they offer a nuclear guarantee of protection to any state signing the treaty that is exposed to nuclear threat by any other state whether or not it signed the NPT.

The cost of adequate inspection, national sensitivities, and other factors have rendered the NPT safeguards less than effective. International inspectors cannot readily discover hidden nuclear facilities. As a matter of fact, the effectiveness of safeguards lies in the political and military intentions of any state that is developing or receiving nuclear technology; it is limited by the extent of the willingness of signatories to the treaty and other countries to avoid using plutonium for atomic weapons. Actually, because it is very difficult for many states to develop nuclear technology on their own, the development of military nuclear weapons might only be avoided by preventing such states from obtaining from abroad fissionable materials which are essential for the development of nuclear weapons.

Even though Israel voted in favor of the NPT, up to the present time it has neither signed nor ratified it. According to *Al-'Askariyah al-Sahyuniyah*, Israel argued that the procedures of verification which the NPT provides for do not rule out acts of espionage.[95] Also, Chari noted that Israel claimed that it did not sign the NPT because it did not provide credible guarantees against nuclear blackmail or nuclear attack. Israel also claimed that it would seek security by preserving a nuclear option to which it could resort at a future time and that its signing of the NPT would deny it this security.[96] Observers of Israeli nuclear strategy have agreed that Israel's lack of commitment to the NPT clearly expresses its desire not to restrict its freedom of action in the field of nuclear weapons development.[97]

FOOTNOTES

1. Simha Plapan, "Nuclear Power in the Middle East," *New Outlook*, Vol. 17, No. 6 (152), July 1974, p. 48; D.K. Palit and P.K.S. Namboodiri, *Pakistan's Islamic Bomb* (New Delhi: Vikas, 1979), p. 46.
2. P.R. Chari, "The Israeli Nuclear Option: Living Dangerously," *International Studies*, Vol. 16, No. 3, July-September 1977, p. 346.
3. Flapan, *op. cit.*, p. 46.
4. Palit and Namboodiri, *op. cit.*, p. 47.

5. Leonard Beaton and John Maddox, *The Spread of Nuclear Weapons* (London: Chatto and Windus for The Institute for Strategic Studies, 1962), p. 174.
6. *The New York Times*, July 18, 1970.
7. Palit and Namboodiri, *op. cit.*, p. 46.
8. *Al-'Askariyah al-Sahyuniyah. Al-Mujallad al-Awwal: Al-Mu'assasah al-'Askariyah al-Isra'iliyah: Al-Nash'ah, al-Tatawwur, 1887-1977* (Al-Qahirah: Markaz al-Dirasat al-Siyasiyah wa-al-Istratijiyah, Mu'assasat al-Ahram, 1972), p. 423.
9. Fuad Jabber, *Israel and Nuclear Weapons: Present Option and Future Strategies* (London: Chatto and Windus for The International Institute for Strategic Studies, 1971), pp. 23, 41-46.
10. William B. Bader, *The United States and the Spread of Nuclear Weapons* (New York: Pegasus, 1968), p. 89.
11. Palit and Namboodiri, *op. cit.*, p. 48.
12. *Al-'Askariyah al-Sahyuniyah, op. cit.*, p. 425.
13. Palit and Namboodiri, *op. cit.*, pp. 47-48.
14. Yusuf Mruwwih, *Al-Abhath al-Dhariyah al-Isra'iliyah* (Beirut: Markaz al-Abhath, 1969), p. 10; Chari, *op. cit.*, p. 347.
15. *Ibid.*
16. *Taqrir al-Mash al- Istratiji 1972.* Ma'had al-Dirasat al-Istratijiyah, translated by B. 'Aql (Beirut: Al-Mu'assasah al-'Arabiyah), p. 156.
17. Chari, *op. cit.*, p. 348.
18. Bader, *op. cit.*, p. 89.
19. *Yisrael-'Arav: Himush o Peruz Atomi* (Tel Aviv: 'Amikam, 1963), p. 92.
20. Palit and Namboodiri, *op. cit.*, p. 49.
21. *Ibid.*
22. *The New York Times*, June 28, July 28, 1966 and July 18, 1970; Todd Friedman, "Israel's Nuclear Option," *Bulletin of the Atomic Scientists*, Vol. 30, No. 7, September 1974, p. 174.
23. *Egyptian Gazette* (Cairo), November 11, 1976.
24. Chari, *op. cit.*, pp. 347-48.
25. Palit and Namboodiri, *op. cit.*, p. 49.
26. Mahmud 'Azmi, "Al-Khayar al-Nawawi al-Isra'ili Darurah Istratijiyah," *Shu'un Filastiniyah*, No. 43, March 1975, p. 94.
27. "Israeli Uranium Method for Peaceful Aims Only," *The Jerusalem Post Weekly*, March 26, 1974.
28. Chari, *op. cit.*, pp. 349-50.
29. *Ibid.*
30. *Ibid.*, p. 346.
31. Bader, *op. cit.*, p. 92.
32. Muhammad H. Heikal, "Atomic Danger on the Middle East Horizon," *New Outlook*, September 1965, p. 56.
33. H. Smith, "U.S. Assumes the Israelis Have A-Bomb or Its Parts," *The New York Times*, July 18, 1970.
34. *Al-Muharrir*, December 3, 1974.
35. Bader, *op. cit.*, p. 92.
36. Mruwwih, *op. cit.*, p. 64.
37. Steve Weissman and Herbert Krosney, *The Islamic Bomb* (New York: Times Books, 1981), p. 107.
38. As cited by Weissman and Krosney, *Ibid.*, p. 108.
39. As cited by Weissman and Krosney, *Ibid.*, p. 109.

Israeli and Arab Nuclear Activities

40. Avigdor Haselkorn, "Israel: From an Option to a Bomb in the Basement," from Robert M. Lawrence and Joel Larus, eds., *Nuclear Proliferation—Phase II* (Lawrence, Kansas: The University Press of Kansas, 1974), pp. 168-69.
41. *Ibid.,* p. 173.
42. *SIPRI Yearbook 1972: World Armament and Disarmament* (Stockholm: International Peace Research Institute, 1972), p. 312.
43. Palit and Namboodiri, *op. cit.,* p. 52.
44. *Al-Ahram,* November 24, 1973.
45. Friedman, *op. cit.,* p. 36.
46. Steven J. Rosen, "Nuclearization and Stability in the Middle East," in Onkar Marwah and Ann Schulz, eds., *Nuclear Proliferation and the Near-Nuclear Countries* (Cambridge, Mass.: Ballinger, 1975), p. 157.
47. *The Jerusalem Post,* November 25, 1975.
48. *Times of India* (New Delhi), March 17, 1976.
49. *The New York Times,* July 18, 1970.
50. *Ma'ariv* (Tel Aviv), July 5, 1971; *Washington Evening Star,* March 22, 1972.
51. *Jane's All the World Aircraft* (London: Jane's Yearbooks), 1970-71, p. 595; 1971-72, p. 536 and 1972-73, p. 565.
52. William Beecher, "Israeli Missile Activity Stirs Conjecture on Atom Weapons," *International Herald Tribune,* October 6, 1971.
53. *Ibid.*
54. *The Times* (London), October 9, 1971.
55. Bader, *op. cit.,* p. 90.
56. Chari, *op. cit.,* p. 350.
57. Robert J. Pranger and Dale R. Tahtinen, *Nuclear Threat in the Middle East* (Washington, D.C.: American Enterprise Institute for Public Policy Research, 1975), pp. 41-42.
58. Mason Willrich and Theodore Taylor, *Nuclear Theft: Risks and Safeguards* (Cambridge: Ballinger, 1974), pp. 5-6.
59. Haselkorn, *op. cit.,* p. 151.
60. Heikal, *op. cit.,* p. 57.
61. Yusuf Mruwwih, *Akhtar al-Taqaddum al-'Ilmi fi Isra'il* (Beirut: Markaz al-Abhath, 1967), pp. 83-84.
62. 'Azmi, *op. cit.,* p. 95.
63. Mruwwih, *op. cit.,* pp. 83-84.
64. 'Azmi, *op. cit.,* p. 96.
65. As cited by Weissman and Krosney, Ibid., p. 302.
66. Gideon Gottleib, "Israel and Atom Bomb," *Commentary,* February, 1961, p. 94.
67. Chari, *op. cit.,* p. 350.
68. J. Bowyer Bell, "Israel's Nuclear Option," *The Middle East Journal,* Vol. 26, No. 4, Autumn, 1972, p. 381.
69. Eliezer Livneh, "Israel Must Come Out for Denuclearization," *New Outlook,* June 1966, p. 45.
70. Chari, *op. cit.,* p. 350.
71. Palit and Namboodiri, *op. cit.,* p. 62.
72. See *Al-Musawwar,* September 23, 1955.
73. *Yisrael-'Arav: Himush o Peruz Atomi, op. cit.,* p. 92.
74. *Al-Ahram,* March 14, 1960.
75. *Ma'ariv,* May 8, 1963.
76. *Yisrael-'Arav: Himush o Peruz Atomi, op. cit.,* p. 93.

77. *Ma'ariv,* April 30, 1963.
78. *International Atomic Energy Agency Bulletin,* Vol. 1, 1959.
79. Shim'on Yiftah, *Ha'idan Hagar'ini Bamizrah Hatikhon* (Tel Aviv: 'Am 'Oved, 1976), p. 71.
80. *Ibid.,* p. 72.
81. *Ibid.*
82. *Ibid.*
83. *Ibid.,* pp. 75-76.
84. *ibid.,* p. 78.
85. *Ibid.*
86. *Ibid.*
87. Chari, *op. cit.,* p. 350.
88. *Action,* June 23, 1980.
89. Weissman and Krosney, *op. cit.,* p. 297.
90. *Ibid.,* pp. 298-99.
91. Willrich and Taylor, *op. cit.,* p. 115.
92. *The Defense Monitor,* Vol. 4, No. 2, February 1975, p. 8.
93. Ralph Lapp, "The Ultimate Blackmail," *The New York Times Magazine,* February 4, 1973, p. 31.
94. Willrich and Taylor, *op. cit.,* p. 25.
95. *Al-'Askariyah al-Sahyuniyah, op. cit.,* p. 425.
96. Chari, *op. cit.,* p. 343.
97. *Al-'Askariyah al-Sahyuniyah, op. cit.,* p. 425.

Chapter II

The Rationale for Israel's Taking a Nuclear Posture

1. Insecurity as a Justification for a Nuclear Option

In Israel, concern over national security takes preeminence over all other matters for the state and the people. Those officially concerned with security matters have encouraged the ascendancy to political power of a military or semi-military group comprising intelligence and military personnel who were involved in the struggle that led to Israel's independence and also groups of intellectuals and politicians who prepared the ground for Israel's establishment and survival.

The following discussion presents some of the more important arguments offered by proponents and opponents in the debate, in Israel and abroad, on the question of Israel's acquisition of nuclear weapons, and describes how they perceive future nuclear developments in the Middle East.

In Israel, there have been two groups with various views concerning the advantages and disadvantages, from the standpoint of Israel's security, of the Israeli nuclear development program and of the introduction of nuclear weapons into the Middle East. Some Israeli political and military decision-makers have been, from the day Israel came into being and in subsequent years, protagonists of the military nuclear option, including the late Israeli Premier and Defense Minister David Ben Gurion, the late Defense and Foreign Minister Moshe Dayan, and former Defense Minister Shim'on Peres. They adopted the French strategic approach according to which "a nuclear deterrent is the only solution to counteract an inferiority in manpower and in the conventional arms race."[1] In reaching their decision, they came to an understanding that, in order to fulfill Israel's goals, no option should be overlooked, and that the acquisition of nuclear weapons is such an option. That is, Israel's sense of external danger encouraged the government to develop a nuclear weapons program. In the Palestine War of 1948, the Jewish community in Palestine established Israel in May 1948 and defeated, at a costly price for the Jewish community, the Arab troops. Nevertheless, it took by force slightly over 80 percent of the land of Palestine. In spite of that, the Israelis did not develop a sense of military security even though they realized that they had won a victory not only because of their military superiority, but also because of the dissensions, the disunity, the near total lack of military cooperation and coordination and the absence of common political objectives among the Arabs.

Muhammad H. Heikal, a confidant of late President Jamal 'Abd al-Nasir and late President Anwar al-Sadat, advanced some of the reasons why Israel has considered the nuclear option. Heikal pointed out that Israel is conscious of its increasing military, material, political, and diplomatic isolation, and that it may one day find itself in circumstances where it will no longer be able to rely on the states which have helped it so far. Heikal further said that Israel has considered the nuclear option as well because it does not have friends or standing among the Afro-Asian states.[2] In addition, although Israel, politically and diplomatically, has greatly benefited from Western support, the Israelis are fearful that they might one day find themselves in circumstances where their Western allies will disengage themselves from their commitments to Israel, a day when the United States and West European states will change their policies towards them in favor of the Arabs. This fear is reinforced by various events such as the attitude taken by the Eisenhower Administration towards the Anglo-French-Israeli invasion of Egypt in 1956, and the United States pressure which was put on Israel to withdraw from Sinai and the Gaza Strip in 1957. In 1956 and 1957, President Dwight Eisenhower threatened to discontinue military and economic assistance to Israel unless it withdrew from these two areas to the international borders. As is known, Israel eventually complied.

During the Suez crisis the Israelis came to realize that France and Britain were no longer the global powers they used to be, and concluded that it could not rely on them for its security. Furthermore, the United States, the staunchest Israeli supporter up to the present time, might one day also lose considerable influence on the international scene. If United States support for Israel were ever reduced or discontinued for whatever reason, Israelis fear that they would be at the mercy of the Arabs, if they have no nuclear arms.

Israel's fears probably have been vindicated by some of the changes that have been made in the foreign policies of some Western states. There are signs that the Western states, especially in Western Europe, are raising some questions about the advisability, from the viewpoint of their national interests, of following a completely pro-Israeli policy and of ignoring Arab—including Palestinian—national and political grievances. Immediately after the invasion of Lebanon in 1982, Israel's support in Western Europe and the United States was stretched to a breaking point.

Some Israelis hold that the emergence of Israeli self-reliance or self-assurance, depending on the acquisition of nuclear weapons, would guarantee for it a high political and strategic status, would enable it to stand on the same level with the powerful states, and would raise it once again to the level of a real partner of the United States after it lost that status in the wake of the October 1973 war when it was forced to ask for the United States airlift to save its conventional military position which had been dangerously threatened. Nuclear weapons, it is argued, would also provide stability for its foreign policy by liberating Israel from the need to rely heavily on the Great Powers to guarantee its existence.[4] Finally, Israel, for the last three decades, was preponderantly dominated by political leaders from Eastern Europe who had experienced political and economic hardships in Eastern and Central Europe during the first half of this century. The world view of these leaders was molded by this experience, which caused them to nurture distrust toward non-Jews. Many Israeli decision-makers still hold the position that they cannot afford to risk placing reliance on others for their security but only upon a superior military capability—including nuclear arms.

Israelis have been afraid that the Arab world could be unified by a charismatic leader who would accelerate Arab modernization politically, socially, economically, and militarily.[5] Israel's fears were intensified by the Egyptian revolution of July 23, 1952, and the increased appeal of Arab nationalism under the leadership of Jamal 'Abd al-Nasir. 'Abd al-Nasir, with Eisenhower's support, had won a political victory after the failure of the British-French-Israeli invasion of Egypt in 1956. Hence, the feeling that 'Abd al-Nasir's leadership might produce a united Arab state in the not-too-distant future to threaten Israel. Consequently, it began feeling the need to secure a military capability of its own, independent, as much as possible, of the protection of any Western state.

One may assume that even social, political and economic modernization of the Arab countries would be instrumental in pushing Israel into the nuclear option. Much has been written about industrialization in Egypt in the 1960s. This process received various evaluations by the Israeli political élite. In his series of lectures on "New Security Policy," Shim'on Peres, chairman of the Labor Party, emphasized that the major threat to Israel is embodied in "Nasirism's alliance with modern technology."[6] The Hebrew newspaper *La-Merhav* on January 6, 1962 under the title "Egyptian Industrialization and Its Dangers to Israel," declared that the major result of this industrialization would be strategic, namely, to destroy Israel and that the motive to destroy Israel was a result and not a cause of industrialization arising from future competition to win markets in Africa. That is, some thought that industrialization would lead to military action against Israel. Adherents to this outlook pointed at the increasing military power of Egypt. For the purpose of preventing a neighboring state from reaching military superiority, these Israeli circles concluded that the guarantee for Israel's security should be based on keeping Arab regimes backward. A different opinion was reflected in the positions taken by individuals such as Dr. Nahum Goldmann, former President of the World Zionist Congress, and D. Hacohen, a former Knesset member. They looked in a positive way at the socioeconomic changes in the developing countries. An Egypt with a modernized population would also serve as a market for Israeli products. This approach was also shared by some top officers in the Israeli Army. In his speech at a press conference in Holon, Israel, Major-General M. 'Amit said that "Israel is in favor of a positive economic and social development of Egypt.... The internal problem in Egypt constitutes at the present a grave danger and as long as this problem is not solved, there will be troubles outside of Egypt."[7]

2. Demographic and Economic Factors

Some Arab states now enjoy unprecedented wealth and a considerable political and diplomatic influence. By contrast, Israel is internationally isolated. Its economic circumstances have exercised an important influence on its position in nuclear development.

Israel has been facing severe economic hardships. German reparations to Jews in Israel and remittances from United States Jews have considerably diminished. It faces a perennial balance of payments deficit. Some markets in Europe have been closed to Israeli commodities because of the Common Market regulations. Its debts are increasing substantially and inflation is very high.

Israel's economic problems are compounded by the fact that it is pursuing a policy of establishing settlements in the Gaza Strip, on the West Bank and on the Golan Heights. Its defense budget is also huge. It is financially difficult for it to acquire conventional military equipment powerful enough to offset that of the Arabs. Because of Israel's heavy economic burden and financial constraints, it cannot keep up the arms race in conventional weapons with Arab states indefinitely.

From the very outset Israelis realized that due to the relatively small size of their state and population and with their limited economic resources, while surrounded by tens of millions of Arabs with vast territories and vast natural resources, they could not afford to fight a long conventional war on a large scale and would always suffer from a strategic weakness.

The continuing development and sophistication of conventional military potential requires huge and increasing amounts of financial and economic resources. Though these rising costs of purchasing or developing conventional weapons economically affect both the Arabs and the Israelis, overall they affect Israel to a much greater degree. Proponents of nuclear weapons therefore argue that Israel's production of such weapons and the guarantee of "comprehensive deterrence," relieve it from enormous expenditures on the development, purchase, and production of conventional arms to preserve an appropriate balance of conventional forces between itself and the Arabs. They state, in support of their position as well, that the military divisions stationed in Western Europe fall short in number of the military divisions of the Soviet Union and the other states of the Eastern Bloc. They believe they must rely on nuclear deterrence. Western Europe's decision to depend on nonconventional arms is not a result of its inability to mobilize additional soldiers nor to provide more conventional defensive equipment. Its decision is a result of economic considerations. The defense of Western Europe with nuclear arms instead of conventional arms, these proponents say, is less costly. Likewise, W. B. Bader noted, many years ago, that, "In purely economic terms, Israel may be forced to develop nuclear weapons."[8] Proponents of a nuclear option claim that the danger which is threatening Israel is greater than that which threatens Western Europe, and the cost of the defense of Israel with conventional arms is proportionally larger than that for Western Europe. Hence, the adoption by Israel of a military strategy based on nuclear weapons is more justified, these proponents argue, than the basing of Western Europe's military strategy on such weapons. However, the acquisition of nuclear weapons may not reduce financial expenditures, due to the fact that conventional arms strength should be maintained for deterrence by means of conventional arms of highly probable clashes between Israel and Arab states. This will be particularly true so long as contending parties refuse to negotiate seriously about Palestinian rights and Israel continues to covet territory from its Arab neighbors.

Israeli proponents of nuclear armament maintain that were Arab-Israeli relations similar to, say, German-French relations nowadays there would not be any need for an Israeli nuclear deterrence. If Israel was certain, they argue, that it could coexist with the Arab world, it would not worry about a sudden Arab attack on it. But since peace with the Arab world is remote, they argue, Israel should depend upon various military means instead of diplomacy to assure its own safety.

Israeli decision-makers, who are of European Jewish origin, are of course well aware of the changing ratio of Western and Oriental Jews in favor of the latter. These leaders are certainly mindful of the probability of Israel's eventual assimilation in the Middle Eastern and North African Arab-Islamic area which surrounds Israel. Heikal is of the view that Israeli decision-makers think that the only way to avoid being overwhelmed by their human and cultural environment is to acquire an atomic armory with which to subdue this environment.[9]

3. Deterrence

As has been discussed earlier, the defendants of a nuclear option think that nuclear arms represent the certain and last guarantee for Israel's security and continued existence in its confrontation with Arab states. Protagonists of a nuclear option for Israel have argued that nuclear weapons are not possessed by Arab states and that it is unlikely that they will acquire them. They argue that even in the event that Arab states do acquire them, Israel's nuclear military advantage would prevent a war and a "balance of terror" or an "absolute" deterrent would be established in the Middle East. This would eliminate an Arab threat based on the accumulation of conventional arms and would make an all-out war in the Middle East improbable.

Some scholars argue that an Israeli nuclear option does strengthen the argument of those Arabs who call for a negotiated peace settlement with Israel, and would bring about an Arab renunciation of all plans for military confrontations and the defeat of Israel. Those who oppose the view that Israel would negotiate in good faith if it were solely in possession of nuclear weapons argue that such acquisition may not necessarily give to Israel such a sense of security.

Some analysts maintain that President al-Sadat's conclusion of a peace treaty with Israel was, at least partially, brought about as a result of Israel's nuclear capability, and that al-Sadat maintained that the continuation of a "no-war-no-peace" situation might lead to an outbreak of war in which Israel would use nuclear weapons. If this is true, it shows that Israel's nuclear capability exerts important political pressure on some Arabs. However, protagonists of Israel's possession of nuclear weapons also argue that Israel cannot use its qualitative advantage (that of a higher level of technology and science) in a conventional arms race because of its small size. This argument implies that Israel may hold nuclear weapons but that the Arabs cannot possess, either by purchase or by development or production, nuclear arms. But perhaps this is erroneous thinking. The vision that Israel alone may possess nuclear armament is not realistic. In the light of the spread of nuclear arms in various parts of the world, it can be safely assumed that the Arabs are on their way to developing nuclear weapons themselves or to acquiring nuclear facilities and fissionable materials. One must conclude that the Israeli acquisition of a nuclear option has forced Arabs to make attempts to acquire nuclear weapons and has alarmed many other medium-sized states in the area.

The acquisition by Israel of nuclear weapons could indeed give it a temporary advantage, but it would not remain the only state in the Middle East with such weapons in long run. That which Israelis call "qualitative advantage" in the fields of science and technology might also be achieved and utilized by the Arabs. That is, one cannot assume that a given people will accept the dominance of others simply because they have acquired some technical advantage.

Addressing himself to this subject, Colonel H. Mustafa, an Arab, wrote in an Iraqi daily that "atomic weapons would serve as a permanent deterrent to the Arabs, and would compel them to avoid provocations... Israel's acquisition of atomic weapons will decrease the value of the conventional weapons in the hands of the Arab armies and the importance of their numerical superiority."[10]

As a result, one of the most dangerous effects of Israel's acquisition of nuclear weapons is that it prompts Arab states to acuire such weapons on their own behalf. It is clear that Arab interest in acquiring nuclear weapons is related to Israel's possession of such weapons. This was indicated to be the case when Egypt's Foreign Minister, Isma'il Fahmi, stated that his country has the scientific capability to develop nuclear weapons and that it would continue making efforts to acquire a nuclear military potential. He further noted that peace would not be maintained as long as Israel has not acceded to the Non-Proliferation Treaty of 1970 and has not abided by its provisions.[11]

... If Israel acquired or exploded a nuclear weapon, Egypt would be duty-bound, in order not to expose its national security to danger, to manutacture or obtain a nuclear weapon.[12]

Heikal also wrote that, as a result of Israel's nuclear armament, Egypt must arm itslef with nuclear weapons in order to protect itself from Israel's nuclear arms.[13] Congruent with this line of thinking is Mahmud 'Azmi's view that Israel's acquisition of such weapons makes it inevitable for Arab states to secure scientific and technical capabilities necessary for the production of nuclear weapons. The Arab states would thereby avoid the risk of exposing themselves to the dangers of Israeli nuclear capability and would prevent the Arabs from finding themselves in an extremely disadvantageous position for a long time, dictated by a nuclear deterrence by the Israelis.[14]

Opponents of Israeli nuclear armaments have been warning that Arabs have begun to believe that they cannot beat Israel in a war with conventional weapons, and that they must acquire nuclear weapons as well. However, if the Arabs gain possession of atomic weapons, it might bring about the belief by the Arabs that they could knock out Israel with a surprise nuclear attack. However, others are of the view that denuclearization of the Arab-Israeli conflict is the only alternative to reliance upon a nuclear strategy in the Middle East by all parties.

Some Israelis early maintained that Arab states would eventually have ambitions to develop nuclear weapons. Because of these projections, these Israelis argued, Israel must develop a nuclear capability as well. Thus, in 1963, Dayan reportedly said that Israel should not be lagging in the Middle Eastern race to develop atomic weapons.[15]

Yigal Allon conveyed a rather different opinion on the nuclear subject in 1970:

Concerning the nuclear balance of terror, the most widely held view, which I shared, was that given the choice between both sides having nuclear weapons to act as a mutual deterrent and both being prevented from laying hands on them, we should definitely prefer a balance of power kept by conventional armaments. There was, however, always the danger that the enemy might eventually develop unconventional weapons, or be supplied with them by some nuclear power. It was therefore essential for Israel to follow closely the development in all the Arab countries, and in Egypt in particular, and at the same time to maintain a high standard of research and technology in the nuclear field on the lines pursued by the developed countries of the world. This was necessary in the first instance for the economic, scientific and political development of the country itself. But it is well known that nowadays the scientific and technological know-how of a country constitutes its potential for the production of nuclear weapons; and if Israel was not to be caught napping she had no alternative but to keep up her potential.[16]

Allon, however, clearly had doubts about the effectiveness of nuclear deterrence. He wrote that, "Israel would be exposed to a fresh danger of the utmost gravity if any Arab country got hold of nuclear bombs, irrespective of whether or not Israel herself possessed similar bombs for retaliatory purposes." The regimes of the Arab states may at any time become "militant, unstable, and irresponsible" and there would be little consolation for Israelis "huddled together in anti-radiation shelters" to know that "they could engage in nuclear retaliation."[17] Avigdor Haselkorn also had doubts about nuclear deterrence. He wrote that "If nuclear weapons were to become part of Middle Eastern arsenals Israel would be faced then and only then with a real threat to its physical existence."[18] Yair Evron noted that "It is most unlikely that an Israeli nuclear option would change either the basic pattern of conflict or the basic strategies employed by the two sides."[19] Simha Flapan, wrote that, "The 'balance of terror' is valid least of all in the Middle East."[20] Also, Nahum Goldmann had stated earlier that, "I see no advantage whatsoever nor any moral or security justification for the manufacture of atomic bombs."[21]

Furthermore, Flapan has suggested that Israelis overreacted to the Arabs' announced intentions to develop atomic weapons, and to the help that India and Yugoslavia reportedly provided Egypt with nuclear technology, along with the purchase of nuclear reactors.[22] As it turned out, the Arabs made little progress in developing atomic weapons by 1963; Israelis had indeed overreacted.

4. Changes in the Military Potential of Arab States

Given the quantitative and qualitative changes in the military powers of the Middle Eastern states, it is probable that Israel will not be capable of winning such victories in future wars as it did in 1948-49, 1956, and 1967. This has already been proven by Israel's major losses in the 1973 war. S. Rosen noted that since October 1973, almost every development is in favor of the Arab states with respect to future military balance. Until 1973, Israel had maintained a superiority in conventional arms over the Arabs. However, the Arabs have increased their economic and military power since then. In the future, the nuclear gap between the two parties might well be narrowed also and even changed in favor of the Arabs, and, as Rosen claims, the Arabs may become capable of defeating Israel on the battlefield.[23] Heikal agrees, and thinks that nuclear weapons are likely to become essential for Israel.[24] However, W. B. Bader maintained in 1968 that the situation favors Israel if it were to employ conventional weapons against any threat from the Arabs, and he has argued that the use of nuclear weapons in the Middle East "would be to Israel's short-range disadvantage if a nuclear race began before the Arabs have closed the conventional weapons gap."[25]

As I have indicated, Israel was aware of the fact that the Arabs could gain military superiority over it if both sides relied upon conventional arms alone. Thus, some Israelis advocated that their country should develop nuclear arms, which would give Israel a more or less permanent advantage over the Arab states. Others argued that it would be less dangerous to all countries if they did not adopt nuclear arms. It is much more difficult to establish a balance in military strength based on nuclear arms than it is to do so with conventional weapons; the destructive power of all the countries involved would be much greater if the balance in strength was to be upset. Furthermore, it would be easier for the Israelis to maintain a military balance with the Arabs if only conventional weaponry was involved. In addition, as has not been mentioned, Israel's possession of nuclear weapons might force the Arabs to ask the Soviet Union to supply atomic weapons to them.

More recently, the idea was proposed that it would be more likely that adversary states, which possessed conventional weapons only, would be more willing to negotiate a settlement than would those that possessed nuclear arms.

Since the arguments supporting or opposing the Israelis' development of nuclear arms were begun, it has been pointed out that Israel has lost a monopoly it once enjoyed in developing or acquiring conventional weapons to equip its army against the Arab states, which did not have access to weapons of the same quality. In addition, it is said that foreign support of Israel is now flagging in favor of the Arabs. For these reasons, some Israelis believe that they must rely upon their own strengths and resources to assure their security; one way to do this is to develop nuclear superiority over any potential enemy.

Moreover, there is a growing number of Western leaders who question the validity of the claim that the West benefits from Israel and who are concerned about Western interests in the Arab lands because of the Western support for Israel. Against this background, Israelis decided, according to some observers, to go nuclear, believing that a nuclear armory could ensure security.

5. Western Influences on Israeli Attitudes

The invariable use by Western and non-Western powers of nuclear weaponry as an "international currency" of power has also influenced Israeli nuclear thinking. Due to Israel's close association with France in the 1950s and the early 1960s, it appears that Israel was considerably influenced by the French strategies based on pre-emption. Probably, one of the theses which had a strong influence on Israel's nuclear thinking was that advanced by the French General Pierre Gallois. In the late 1950s, France witnessed a heated debate on the question whether or not it should produce nuclear weapons or should depend on the United States nuclear arsenal. Gallois advanced the argument that the strategic objectives of a state like France do not necessarily correspond to those of a great power like the United States, and that the United States would not necessarily be a credible power that would guarantee the security of France in a situation where Western Europe alone was facing a nuclear threat.

Due to their close association with the United States it seems that the Israelis were also greatly influenced by United States strategies based on pre-emption. The Americans during the 1950s gave popularity to the thesis that the threat of first use of nuclear arms can serve as a deterrent to a state possessing superior conventional weapons. This thesis has been invalidated in cases, like the Soviet-American one, where both sides have nuclear arms. The thesis is valid in cases where one side does not possess such weapons, even if it is superior in conventional weaponry, as in the Israeli-Arab case.

During the Suez war of 1956, the Soviet Union threatened to use nuclear rockets against the invading powers of France and Britain. Regardless of the credibility of the threat, it is highly probable that the threat left an impact on Israeli nuclear conduct. Israel probably reached a conclusion that, with nuclear arms, it would be able to exert deterrence not only with respect to the Arabs but, to a certain extent, with respect to nuclear-armed states such as the U.S.S.R. that might decide to intervene on the side of Arab states in any future Arab-Israeli hostilities.

The argument that Israel should develop nuclear weapons and equip its armed forces with them was enhanced in 1973. In June 1967, the army had easily invaded Arab land. In the October 1973 war the Israeli army had suffered serious setbacks, however, against the Egyptian and Syrian forces. Fearing, as well, that foreign military support would be required in any future wars, especially if they turned out to be prolonged, Israeli decision-makers considered the possibility of equipping the armed forces with nuclear weapons. Opponents to this policy once again claimed that the Arabs would turn to the Soviet Union, with a concomitant expansion of Soviet influence in the Middle East, to obtain similar arms. Opponents of a nuclear option, however, argue that the preservation of its military superiority and the United States full guarantee of its existence and security would give Israel the assurance it needed to dispense with the production of nuclear arms. (The accuracy of this argument is very questionable in that United States policy supporting Israel has changed, especially with respect to the Arab states and the Palestine question).

Opponents of nuclear weapons argue that Israel's acquisition of nuclear deterrence, with the concomitant endeavor by Arab states to acquire the same capability before Israel could carry out the Zionist goal of establishing national "Greater Israel" constitutes a great danger to the achievement of this goal. Furthermore, Israel's success in creating a state of comprehensive deterrence through nuclear arms would not be very effective against any guerrilla-type warfare that the Palestinians might wage.

6. Committee for Nuclear Disarmament of the Arab-Israeli Region

In 1961 a small group was formed in Israel, called the Committee for Nuclear Disarmament of the Arab-Israeli Region, that claimed that any government effort to develop nuclear weapons would be a waste of national means and valuable scientific resources. The Committee also deplored the secrecy with which a few Israeli government officials had pursued policies involving nuclear energy without informing the public or the Knesset.

Members of the Committee maintained that nuclear armament in the Middle East is an area of concern which has a considerable significance and threat for all people and that public opinion should have been considered. The Committee's members were convinced during its early days that the North Atlantic-Soviet rapprochement would be followed by pressure to discourage the spread of nuclear weapons. They believed that Israel should take the initiative and demand demilitarization of the Middle East from nuclear arms with sufficient guarantees.

In April 1962 the Committee demanded that the countries of the Middle East refrain from manufacturing nuclear arms by mutual agreement. The United Nations should supervise the area in order to prevent production of nuclear weapons. Also, Middle Eastern countries would be denied the ability to acquire nuclear weapons from other states.[26] The Committee, however, was unable to pressure or persuade the Knesset and the government of Israel to accept its views.

FOOTNOTES

1. Simha Flapan, "Nuclear Power in the Middle East," *New Outlook*, Vol. 17, No. 6 (152), July 1974, p. 49.
2. Muhammad H. Heikal, "Atomic Danger on the Middle East Horizon," *New Outlook*, September, 1965, pp. 54-57.
3. D.K. Palit and P.K.S. Namboodiri, *Pakistan's Islamic Bomb* (New Delhi: Vikas, 1979), p. 46.
4. *Al-'Askariyah al-Sahyuniyah. Al-Mujallad al-Awwal: Al-Mu'assasah al-'Askariyah al-Isra'iliyah: Al-Nash'ah, al-Tatawwur, 1887-1977* (Al-Qahirah: Markaz al-Dirasat al-Siyasiyah wa-al-Istratijiyah, Mu'assasat al-Ahram, 1972), pp. 424-25.
5. Flapan, *op. cit.*., p. 48.
6. *Davar*, October 15, 1962.
7. *La-Merhav*, August 19, 1963.
8. William B. Bader, *The United States and the Spread of Nuclear Weapons* (New York: Pegasus, 1968), p. 91.
9. Heikal, *op. cit.*
10. From a series of articles written by a retired colonel in January 1961 in the Baghdad daily *Al-Ahali*. Translated into English by Avraham Ben-Tzur, "The Arabs and the Israeli Reactor," *New Outlook*, March-April 1961, p. 21.
11. Flapan, *op. cit.*, pp. 47-48.
12. "Fahmy Warns: Egypt Would Make A-Bomb," *The Jerusalem Post Weekly*, June 18, 1974.
13. Heikal, *op. cit.*, p. 57.
14. Mahmud 'Azmi, "Al-Khayar al-Nawawi al-Isra'ili Darurah Istratijiyah," *Shu'un Filastiniyah*, No. 43, March 1975, p. 99.
15. *The New York Times*, April 13, 1963.
16. Yigal Allon, *The Making of Israel's Army* (London: Vallentine Mitchell, 1970), pp. 69-70.
17. *Ibid.*, pp. 78, 112.
18. Avigdor Haselkorn, "Israel: From an Option to a Bomb in the Basement," from Robert M. Lawrence and Joel Larus, eds., *Nuclear Proliferation-Phase II* (Lawrence, Kansas: The University Press of Kansas, 1974), p. 165.
19. Yair Evron, "Israel and the Atom: The Uses and Misuses of Ambiguity, 1957-1967." *Orbis*, Vol. 17, No. 4., Winter 1974, pp. 1332-33, 1342.
20. Flapan, *op. cit.*, p. 54.
21. A statement by Dr. N. Goldmann, endorsed by Yigal Yadin, former Chief of Staff of the Israel Defense Army and former Deputy Prime Minister, and other eminent Israelis in the Hebrew daily *Ma'ariv* interview. Translated in "The Atom Bomb in Israel: A Symposium," *New Outlook*, March-April 1961, p. 15.
22. Flapan, *op. cit.*, p. 53.

23. Steven J. Rosen, "Nuclearization and Stability in the Middle East," in Onkar Marwah and Ann Schulz, eds., *Nuclear Proliferation and the Near-Nuclear Countries* (Cambridge, Mass.: Ballinger, 1975), p. 166.
24. Heikal, *op. cit.*, pp. 54-57.
25. Bader, *op. cit.*, p. 93.
26. Committee for Nuclear Disarmament of the Arab-Israeli Region, "Keep Nuclear Weapons Out of Our Region," *New Outlook,* Vol. 9, July-August 1966, pp. 64-65.

Chapter III

Arab-Israeli Nuclear Dynamics

1. Some Explanations of the Israeli Development of Nuclear Weapons

Some students of the Arab-Israeli conflict, such as Haselkorn, are of the view that the instability of the Arab-Israeli interrelations arises from the fact that Arab states have always maintained the strategic initiative. This, according to Haselkorn, posed a dilemma to the Israelis: Either resign themselves to the fact that the Arabs have gained the upper hand in the balance of power, or deny it and use force to avoid their gaining it. He is of the view that Israelis must follow the second course and develop nuclear weapons.[1] Perhaps, however, Haselkorn and other students of nuclear weapons affairs related to the Middle East have been under the influence of the Super Powers which support a theory of bipolar deterrence and the manufacture of nuclear weapons to counter nuclear threat.

Four arguments have been put forth to explain why Israel developed nuclear weapons. The first might be called the anticipatory argument, "It was generally assumed that Israel would not go from the nuclear option to the nuclear bomb itself without a very pressing sense of insecurity. The inhibitions were thought to be too powerful, the dangers of pre-emptive attack too great... But this was always a weak argument simply because, if the dangers of pre-emptive attack were so real, Israel was more likely to make the bomb in an hour of triumph than in a period of insecurity. Now [immediately after the June 1967 war] the hour of triumph has come but... Israel might still feel a sense of long term insecurity. Now, if ever, is the time to go ahead."[2] The second is the technical-strategic argument. This argument proposes that "Israel should be capable of assembling at least a crude device; it may have what is termed "turnkey" capability. It has the means of delivery ... required for the distances that may be involved...." Also, "Because of Israel's special security situation, including its vulnerable geographic position, a few crude, even untested, nuclear weapons which could be delivered over short distances is all that might be required in another all-out war with the Arabs in which Israel was threatened with being overrun."[3] The third could be called the instrumental argument. Following the June 1967 war it was argued that nuclear weapons would "be much more relevant now that the conventional warfare alternative has apparently fallen short of securing an adequate long term solution to [Israel's] basic political and security problems."[4] Furthermore, some analysts maintain that nuclear weapons may not only be viewed by Israel's leadership in terms of ultimate deterrence but... also as an instrument that can effectively contribute to the realization of desired foreign policy or security objectives in a manner that conventional military superiority has not. Finally, there is the political dynamics argument. It contends that "with the fluid and violent nature of Middle Eastern politics and the undependable shifts and initiatives of the great powers involved, if Israel were to have a nuclear weapons capability on call and yet not 'formally' possess the weapons, the lead time for completion would have to be most brief to be of any serious use in a bargaining process that might begin almost without notice... Israel must either have atomic weapons or not."[5]

Acquisition of nuclear weapons by one or more states would create strong fears and suspicions about the political and military goals of these states. Since Israel and those Arab states that might come to possess nuclear weapons cannot be sure when and under what precise circumstances they might be a target of nuclear attack, and since there is no mutual confidence between the two parties, there is a real likelihood that Israel or an Arab state (or more than one Arab state) strike first with nuclear weapons in order to get rid of the burden of uncertainty about the real intentions of the other party. Various Arab states, if they came to possess nuclear weapons, most certainly would have different attitudes and views on the use of these weapons against nuclear Israel. We can assume a situation in which some Arab states would refrain from employing their nuclear arms against Israel, but some other Arab states might be ready to regain Arab lands and under special circumstances, to wage atomic war against Israel if they thought that they could destroy the state of Israel, even at the cost of a very high price in terms of human lives and material.

2. Nuclear Policy Alternatives

First, a state could adopt a policy based on the alternative, called *positive certainty*, by which it would make it known that it had fabricated nuclear arms, although in reality it had not. This, obviously, would be a bluff to enhance *deterrence* of enemy attack. As with any bluff, the effectiveness of the policy would depend on whether or not anybody believed that that state possessed nuclear weapons. This policy suffers shortcomings in that if the bluff was believed, it would encourage enemy states to acquire nuclear weapons. If the bluff was discovered, that state's credibility in the eyes of the world would be diminished. Second, a state could develop a policy based on the alternative of *negative certainty* by which it would declare that it would not try to develop the capacity to produce nuclear weapons. This policy might contribute to discouraging enemy states from developing nuclear weapons, but it also would mean that that state had sacrificed a bargaining tool and also a deterrent from conventional attack. Finally, a policy, which could be called *uncertainty-ambiguity*, could be chosen by which a state would show that it was "neutral" in its approach to develop nuclear arms. This has the advantage of preserving that state's option to acquire nuclear weapons if events indicated that it should do so.

In fact, Israel has pursued a policy of uncertainty and shrouded in secrecy its nuclear weapons program. Official Israeli policy on the nuclear issue might be summarized as follows. Israel has a nuclear option. The terms employed in the official Israeli position are ambiguous and, hence, they are a source of uncertainty. However, Israelis have gone so far as to say that Israel "would not be the first" to introduce nuclear weapons into the Middle East, as Premier Eshkol had stated.[6] Israel has taken this official position in order to check any criticism which would surely be forthcoming if it asserted bluntly that it had a stockpile of nuclear weapons.

It is not clear what is meant by statements to the effect that Israel will not be the first to introduce nuclear weapons into the Middle East. Such statements could be interpreted in various ways as denoting that Israel will not be the first "to bomb," "to deploy," "to test," "to produce," etc. Moreover, the pledge not to be the first to introduce nuclear weapons into the Middle East "leaves some ambiguities which hardly renounce Israeli bomb programs, since nuclear weapons have already been introduced into the Middle East on board ships of the American Sixth Fleet and very possibly on board Soviet ships in the Mediterranean."[7] And further, "it is highly unlikely that the Israelis will wait until Egypt starts exercising the [nuclear] option and their considerable lead time is expended before they consider that nuclear weapons have been introduced and start their own arms production."[8]

One can assume that the Arabs and the Israelis are expecting the worst possible conduct from each other. If this assumption is correct, each party would be expected to be developing nuclear weapons because each party is expecting that the other party is doing the same. Consequently, the commitment by one party not to be the first to employ nuclear weapons is not convincing. All such pledges would be disregarded under perceived conditions or circumstances of despair. Relevant to this point is Karl von Clausewitz's assertion that, "In war more than anywhere else in the world, things happen differently to what we had expected, and look differently when near to what they did at a distance."[9] The statement that "Israel will not be the first to introduce nuclear weapons into the Middle East" implies that Israel would develop its own nuclear arms if some other state did bring these arms into the region, thereby Israel would not be accused of having been the first to introduce nuclear weapons into the Middle East.

Following the policy of uncertainty, Israel refused to agree to an offer made by President 'Abd al-Nasir of Egypt to place the nuclear reactor at Anshas under United Nations safeguards if Israel would do the same with the Dimona reactor. But Israel has persisted in preserving its freedom of action at the Dimona reactor. Israel also has refused to accede to the Non-Proliferation Treaty, arguing that various political, economic, industrial, and defense considerations prevent it from agreeing to accession.[10] This attitude, in the 1960s, also tended to serve Israel's policy of nuclear uncertainty by causing Arab states to wonder whether Israel really did have nuclear weapons or was drawing nearer to acquiring them. But in the 1970s, particularly after many leaks in the 1973 war, no sophisticated Arab government doubts that Israel possesses the bomb.

By keeping an open nuclear option—and maintaining at the same time an ambiguous nuclear policy—Israel came to enjoy the advantage of having an option to develop nuclear weapons whenever it wanted to and without the embarrassment of submitting to inspection. By employing a policy of ambiguity, it has sought to exert an influence on decision-makers of Arab states or simply to intimidate them. That is, by attempting to conceal its exact nuclear intentions and capabilities, Israel deters Arab states from launching war against it and from acquiring nuclear weapons. For example, former Israeli Prime Minister Ben Gurion, in explaining the Dimona facility to the Knesset after the press discovered its existence, described it as a scientific institute for research in problems of arid zones and desert flora and fauna. He also labeled reports that Israel is constructing an atomic device as either a deliberate or an unconscious untruth. Ben Gurion's answer to a question of whether or not Israel is interested in atomic energy and atomic arms is a reflection of this policy of sowing doubt. Ben Gurion's reply was, "... in atomic energy—yes; in atomic arms—not yet."[11]

Ben Gurion held a discussion on the Dimona reactor with S. Sulzberger, a senior political correspondent of *The New York Times*. After the discussion, Sulzberger wrote that Ben Gurion hinted with anger that Israel might be engaged at the Dimona nuclear reactor in nuclear research for military purposes. Ben Gurion announced in April 1963 that after several years Israel would become a nuclear power.[12]

In *The Jerusalem Post*, an article, appearing on May 28, 1963, stated that, thanks to a more advanced stage of technology and to the existence of a reactor for research purposes, Israel was considered nearer to nuclear capability. In 1966 it was reported that Israel already had French-made Diamant missiles. Its acquisition of such missiles raised questions about its nuclear intentions because such a missile has little military importance in a conventional program but is of great military value when carrying a warhead of great destructive power.

In July 1966, a debate took place in the Knesset between some leftist members and some ministers on nuclear disarmament in the Middle East and on Israel's precise position on nuclear armament. Shim'on Peres, who then was a member of the Party of the Workers of the Land of Israel (MAPAI) and who has been calling for Israel's acquisition of nuclear weapons, said that he saw no reason for Israel to let 'Abd al-Nasir know what the Israelis do and do not do, that he knew that the Arabs doubted Israel's nuclear intentions and that doubt had a deterrent power.[13] Peres said: Why should we alleviate these doubts and why should we clarify them? He remarked that it is not in the interest of Israel to dispel Arab fears.[14]

By Israel's raising the level of Arab doubts as to its nuclear capability, Israeli decision-makers may believe that Arab political elites may become less opposed to Israel's plans for a political settlement, or, as a consequence of Arab doubts, they may believe that Arab moral power might become shaken and the Arab will to regain the territories which Israel has occupied since June 1967 might be weakened. In fact, as the 1973 war demonstrated, Arab leaders have not been intimidated by this Israeli approach.

The Israelis probably decided to admit that they had the capability to make atomic weapons because they felt that a policy of uncertainty was not bringing about the desired effects, as the 1973 war demonstrated. Israel decided to try this new policy to see if that would have a deterrent effect. However, it has not been determined absolutely that this policy will work either.

Assuming that a nuclear military balance would be established at some time in the future between Israel and Arab states, if such a balance is at all possible, how stable would it be? With the assumption that nuclear weapons are in the hands of both Israel and the Arab states, the danger posed by nuclear weapons in a Middle East conflict situation is very great indeed.

3. Scenarios of Employment of Nuclear Weapons

Some of the probable scenarios in which nuclear weapons might be employed in the Middle East can be based on analogous military operations involving conventional forces by states with military strength comparable to that of Middle Eastern states. For example, it is known that India has exploded a nuclear device. If a conventional war broke out between India and Pakistan and Pakistan got the upper hand by using conventional arms and India then used tactical nuclear weapons, we would have a situation comparable to Israeli use of the bomb. One can assume that nuclear weapons would be employed by one or more Middle Eastern states under certain circumstances, such as desperation or the perceived need for a more forceful military response than conventional weapons can achieve. If one power was threatened with defeat on the battlefield, by another country's conventional forces, the weight of world public opinion with regard to the decision to employ nuclear weapons would differ from one state to another. Given the sociopolitical and national climate and dynamics in the Middle East, it is probable that nuclear weapons would be employed in that area in a number of situations, not only that of a last-ditch defensive posture, although, obviously, the latter would be the best pretext for using nuclear weapons.

One probable scenario of the employment of nuclear weapons in the Middle East is related to the question of national survival; that is, the situation in which a state is making a last-ditch effort to defend itself against an enemy that is stronger in conventional weaponry. If one state has nuclear weapons, then its use of these weapons is the only alternative to surrender and occupation by another state. The survival syndrome seems to be a permanent feature in the Middle East. For Israel, this finds its expression in anxiety over a Jewish holocaust. Pranger and Tahtinen pointed out that, "A corollary to this fixation is the so-called 'Masada complex,' a state of mind in Israel that would resist national capitulation until the last defender."[15]

Fear of the holocaust and the idea of a Masada-like resistance to national capitulation may be rooted in Israeli political and military decision-making bodies in spite of Israel's military victories in its wars with Arab states. However, Arab states have fears over their national security and survival which Israel has created. These fears are reinforced by Israel's military strength as manifested in its military victories over the Arabs from 1948 until the present time and Israel's acquisition of Arab lands. Israel's parliament in 1980 formally annexed East Jerusalem and its environs, and in 1981 extended Israel's jurisdiction, laws, and administration to the Golan Heights. Today, much doubt is expressed among experts that Israel will readily withdraw from south Lebanon. The government of Israel apparently still has territorial ambitions with regard to Arab lands. Witnessing or sensing that, Arab states might become convinced, if they have not already been, that peaceful means are not a guarantee to their security and to the recovery of lands recently lost and that war is the only alternative.

Parallel to the Arabs' despair of ever recovering their ancestral lands through peaceful means would be an Israeli awareness that Arabs would certainly turn to a military alternative to regain the lands. Treating this subject, Pranger and Tahtinen noted that, "a new war in the Middle East would probably be interpreted by both sides as something of a final test—like two boxers struggling near the fifteenth round with a feeling that up to this point the match had been a draw."[16] Consequently, a new military confrontation between Israel and some Arab states would generate great anxieties related to real or imagined vital national interests. Hence, nuclear or other unconventional weapons might be employed in such a war. Under certain political, military, and psychological circumstances, it is clear that warring parties in the Middle East do not heed international pressure not to resort to the use of unconventional weapons. As Pranger and Tahtinen pointed out, "In a sense, nuclear war could erupt at any time in a fifth round of fighting between Israel and the Arab states because the enemy would be *figuratively*, if not literally, at the capital gates."[17] Sooner or later, most vital population, industrial, and other centers in the Middle East, including those within Israel, would be threatened with annihilation. In a situation of military confrontation between Israel and Arab states, at a given point, survival would be perceived of as being at stake. At that point—and political decision-makers in the states involved would decide when it is reached—the survival scenario would apply.

Another scenario is concerned with interdiction, in which a state is being attacked, whether by surpirse or not, by another state. The state being attacked would not be able to ward off the attack through the use of conventional weapons. In this situation the state under attack would resort to the use of nuclear weapons if it had them. Also, because of relatively short distances in the Middle East and the considerable increase of the numbers of tanks, artillery pieces, and other weapons in both the Arab and Israeli armies, the parties to the conflict may deem it necessary to resort to a nuclear interdiction strike.

One of the lessons of the October 1973 war is very relevant to a future war in the Middle East. Losses in human lives and equipment on both sides during that war were tremendous and swift. In a more sophisticated war, swifter and higher losses would occur as they have most recently in Lebanon. It is doubtful that the Super Powers allied with the contending states would be able to airlift equipment speedily enough and in sufficient quantities to replenish that which would be destroyed. In such circumstances, one or more parties to a future Middle Eastern war might resort to nuclear weapons.

Like past Arab-Israeli military confrontations, the Lebanese war exemplified some elements of surprise and/or breakthrough. Because of the many and more sophisticated weapons that were used in this war and of the intensity of political positions, moves by one party were of such a proportion that they were considered by the other party as strategically threatening. But in 1982, it became clear that the Arabs, while deeply threatened, had no conventional or nuclear means to deter the attack.

Another probable nuclear scenario is the preventive one in which a state would plan an attack with a strong military force on another state. A state that comes under the threat of attack would launch a preemptive nuclear strike. This scenario implies that in dire circumstances, employment of nuclear weapons could compensate for inferiority in conventional military strength. A preemptive strike might take place when intelligence reports conclude that an enemy is preparing to strike first and in such a way as to reduce the chance to drive him back by conventional weapons.

In a sense, any preemptive war is a form of surprise attack. The effects of a preemptive strike are the same as a surprise attack. Preemptive and surprise attacks seek to catch the enemy off guard. One can assume that a state so attacked would take strong action against the aggressor, who would assume that the attack could be met this way; thus, the attacking country would launch such a devastating surprise attack that it would eliminate the probability of a retaliatory action. Out of fear that an opponent state would launch an attack first and that the attacked party might become inferior militarily, the would-be attacked party might preemptively use nuclear weapons against the opponent state. However, state A, fearing that state B would retaliate with nuclear weapons if attacked with conventional weapons, might decide to launch its preemptive attack with nuclear weapons.

Soviet military engagement in Egypt in 1970 and an Israeli assumption that the Soviet Union might have knowledge about the real state of the Israeli nuclear option might have pushed Israel to manufacture nuclear bombs. It is probably correct to say that if a state has only a short lead time in which to fabricate a nuclear weapon, then the risks of preemption by an enemy state are higher than if that state has a long lead time. Consequently, a state that has a short lead time might decide to go nuclear since it would run higher risks of being struck by an enemy preemptive strike. Haselkorn claimed that this situation faced Israel in 1970.[18]

Because of the relatively short distances between strategic targets in the Middle East, the warning time in case of a nuclear attack is very short; it would be difficult to protect air fields upon which retaliatory strikes would be made; the intervening period between the launching of one nuclear rocket and a full nuclear confrontation, probably culminating in total nuclear destruction, would therefore be much smaller. All these factors place Middle Eastern parties to a conflict under a strong urge or temptation to preempt an enemy attack by launching a nuclear strike.

The temptation to preempt is more powerful in the Middle East than elsewhere due to the successful surprise attacks in the 1967 and 1973 Arab-Israeli wars. All of these points lead to the conclusion that, whereas nuclear arms have brought about a sort of stability of 'mutual terror' between the big powers, their introduction into the Middle East only serves to aggravate the present instabilities. Pranger and Tahtinen, however, pointed out that it is improbable that "nuclear weapons would be used by anyone out of sheer cunning and with the objective of totally destroying an enemy in a surprise attack...."[19]

There are other scenarios in which nuclear weapons might be used by Israel. An unequal situation in terms of quality and quantity currently holds between Israel and the Arab states. Clearly, Israel has enjoyed quantitative superiority in equipment and arms over each of the Arab states. Its mobilized manpower has been considerable vis-a-vis that of all the Arab states combined; in the 1973 war, however, the Arab states began to reach the point of parity or superiority over Israel in terms of manpower, arms, and equipment, although the qualitative technological gap between the Israelis and the Arabs in favor of the first is still wide. Even this advantage, however, might be narrowing and will perhaps close in the future and the quantitative gap between both sides will perhaps widen in favor of the Arabs.

The former President of the World Zionist Organization (WZO), Nahum Goldmann, stated in 1970,

... At the moment and probably for some time to come, the qualitative superiority of Israel is outstanding; it is unrealistic, however, to rely on it forever; the Arab people have created a brilliant civilization in the past and will no doubt acquire the technological know-how of the West, both in peaceful endeavors and in warfare.[20]

The increase in the number of Israelis killed in military action may be taken as proof of these changes. In the 1956 Sinai war, Israelis claim that less than 300 Israelis were killed; in the June 1967 war, according to Israeli sources, around 600 were killed; in the 1973 October war, according to the same sources, over 3,500 were killed. Israeli deaths in the invasion of Lebanon ar still mounting. As a proof of this argument might also be the fact that whereas Israel's military victory in the June 1967 war was overwhelming, the Arabs initially scored significant military gains and showed progress in their technological skills in the October 1973 war.

What position will Israel take when the nuclear deterrence strategy which it is pursuing proves to be ineffective and when it becomes convinced that its victory in a future war with conventional weapons is not sure any longer? The position that Israel might take in this eventuality or in other strategic, political and military circumstances conceived by Israel as threatening to its national interests would be to resort to use of nuclear weapons against Arab states.

This probability, of course, exists now before Arab states acquire nuclear arms. This possibility would be made less probable if the territories occupied by Israel in the June 1967 war were returned to the Arabs as a means for a political settlement. One of the factors that make this probability higher is the volatility of the situation in the Middle East in social, ideological, political, economic, and military terms.

It is highly probable that in a Middle East where Israel and some Arab states possess nuclear arms, Israel would launch a nuclear preemptive strike against a number of sensitive Arab targets if it, under given Middle Eastern and world circumstances, comes to the conclusion that the Arabs are poised to launch a nuclear strike to eliminate Israel as a viable military, political and demographic entity.

In the absence of a political settlement and in a state of Israeli-Arab equality in modern and advanced conventional weaponry, or even in a condition of Israeli conventional weapons superiority, some Arab governments might try to fulfill their political and naional objectives by one of the various forms of warfare. Israel, thus, might use nuclear arms if it were attacked by Arab states with conventional weapons which either caused a considerable number of casualties or threatened perceived vital Israeli interests.

The nature of an Israeli reaction to an Arab attack also depends upon the number and fire power of Arab troops taking part in the military operations, on the number of Arab states participating in the war and their location (for example, whether Jordan with its long borders with Israel is taking part in the war); it also depends on whether or not the Arabs surprised Israel by such a war.

Another circumstance in which Israel might use nuclear weapons is a protracted military confrontation or a long war of attrition. During such a war, Israel would experience very severe economic difficulties and heavy loss of life. Israel's manpower resources would be absorbed by military needs, causing a shortage of manpower in the economic field. It is doubtful whether Israel during a war of attrition which lasted several months would continue to use conventional weapons without resorting to some sort of nuclear weapons. Israeli generals have stated a number of times that Israel will not fight another war of attrition such as the one in 1969 and 1970, which was costly for the Israelis in terms of lives and money. If a protracted military confrontation would be repeated by the Arabs, Israel would probably decide on a strategic attack involving the use of nuclear weapons.

Israel may resort to the use of nuclear weapons as a solution to its military, political, and economic problems even in a no-war-no-peace situation. Israel has to spend enormous amounts of money on conventional arms in order to match the Arabs. Whatever the Israelis spend on the purchase of conventional arms, they cannot kep up with the Arabs. Furthermore, Arab states are becoming increasingly stronger politically due to their location, numbers, markets, size of their lands, and, most importantly, their petroleum and petrodollars. Arab petroleum and capital are needed more than ever before by many countries and especially by Western Europe, the United States and Japan.

Recent developments described above place greater pressure on Western Europe and the United States to change their policies towards the Arabs regarding the Palestinian question and Israel. We are witnessing the beginning of a change in West European policies and we might be witnessing also an adjustment in the United States policy towards the states of the Middle East. If, as a result of rising Arab influence, the United States and Western Europe adopt a policy calling for Israeli withdrawal from the West Bank, the Gaza Strip, and the Golan Heights and the establishment of a Palestinian state on the West Bank and the Gaza Strip, together with the probable narrowing of the qualitative gap and the widening of the quantitative gap in armaments, then the waging of a prolonged diplomatic and political campaign against Israel by the Arab states, the United States, and Western Europe might also lead Israel to resort to nuclear weapons.

FOOTNOTES

1. Avigdor Haselkorn, "Israel: From an Option to a Bomb in the Basement," from Robert M. Lawrence and Joel Larus, eds., *Nuclear Proliferation—Phase II* (Lawrence, Kansas: The University Press of Kansas, 1974), pp. 149-50.
2. P. Windsor, "The Middle East and the World Balance," *World Today,* July 1967, p. 281.
3. *SIPRI Yearbook 1972: World Armament and Disarmament* (Stockholm: International Peace Research Institute, 1972), p. 312.
4. Fuad Jabber, "Israel's Nuclear Option," *Journal of Palestine Studies,* Autumn 1971, p. 22.
5. J. Bowyer Bell, "Israel's Nuclear Option," *The Middle East Journal,* Vol. 26, No. 4, Autumn 1972, p. 383.
6. *SIPRI Yearbook 1972: World Armament and Disarmament, op. cit.*
7. George H. Quester, "Israel and the Nuclear Non-Proliferation Treaty," *Bulletin of the Atomic Scientists,* Vol. 25, June 1969, p. 44.
8. Jabber, *op. cit,* p. 123.
9. Karl von Clausewitz, *On War,* Book III, Chapter VII, translated by J. J. Graham, 1908, edited by Anatol Rapoport (Baltimore: Penguin Books, 1968), p. 263.
10. *Davar,* January 10, 1969.
11. *Ma'ariv,* February 24, 1963.
12. *Davar,* December 2, 1980.
13. Yisrael-'Arav: Himush o Peruz Atomi, op. cit., p. 151.
14. *Davar,* December 2, 1980.

15. Robert J. Pranger and Dale R. Tahtinen, *Nuclear Threat in the Middle East* (Washington, D.C.: American Enterprise Institute for Public Policy Research, 1975), p. 42.
16. *Ibid.*
17. *Ibid.*, p. 44.
18. Haselkorn, *op. cit.*, p. 169.
19. Pranger and Tahtinen, *op. cit.*, p. 39.
20. N. Goldmann, "The Future of Israel," *Foreign Affairs* 48: 3, April 1970, p. 447.

Chapter IV

Other Risks Leading to Nuclear War

1. Palestinian Guerrilla Organizations and Nuclear Weapons

The probability of organizations, like the Palestinian guerrilla organizations, acquiring nuclear weapons creates uncertainty in the politics of the Israelis and the Arabs.

The Palestine Liberation Organization (PLO), under the leadership of Yasir 'Arafat, is the umbrella organization of the Palestinian guerrilla organizations. The constituent groups of the PLO are represented on the Palestinian Naitonal Council. Power becomes more concentrated at the level of the Central Committee and the Executive Committee chaired by 'Arafat. Within the PLO, the Palestine Liberation Movement (FATH) is the biggest and most powerful guerrilla organization. Next after FATH is the Popular Front for the Liberation of Palestine (PFLP), headed by Dr. George Habash in which are merged two smaller groups, the Heroes of the Return and the Palestinian faction of the Movement of Arab Nationalists. There are at least three groups that originally were part of the PFLP: The Popular Democratic Front for the Liberation of Palestine, headed by Nayif Hawatimih; the Za'rur group; and the Jibril group. The PLO also includes the Syrian-backed al-Sa'iqah.

It is possible that Palestinian guerrilla organizations will acquire nuclear capability from weapon-grade plutonium from various foreign countries. How would Israel react to a nuclear threat from the PLO? Of relevance in the study of relations between states or between states and other political organizations is the value which a political organization places on the achievement of certain political, national, economic, or social objectives. Such objectives might weigh so heavily that political organizations (including states) become insensitive to the kinds of threats of retaliation that lie at the heart of the doctrine of deterrence. The sense of injustice may force a national group to desperate acts of retaliation. For example, if a given Palestinian guerrilla organization were to obtain nuclear weapons and to consider the prospect of using them, the extent of its fear of an Israeli nuclear strike would depend on the dominance of the national and political objectives to which this guerrilla organization subscribes. The dominance of such objectives might be such that the organization would exclude from its calculations the possibility of an Israeli nuclear response. The blocking of some modicum of justice for a national cause may, as in the past, lead to untold disasters for all.

2. Technical Factors Related to the Employment of Nuclear Weapons

A nuclear war can break out by accident. Such a war might occur as a result of technical or human failure: There is no perfect machine and the judgment of any human being can be or become faulty. Radar messages might be misinterpreted. A state, under the erroneous impression that it is the target of a nuclear attack by a certain state, might launch a preemptive nuclear strike against the perceived enemy. Reconnaissance flights, being carried out by one state on or near the territory of other state, might be interpreted by the other state as an act of war and might lead the latter to launch a nuclear weapon.

Since the distances between, say, Israel and Syria or Israel and Iraq are relatively small, a real or imagined threat of nuclear attack would be reponded to quickly. On June 7, 1981, the Iraqi nuclear facilities, for example, were destroyed reportedly by the Israeli airplanes which had to fly about one thousand kilometers. If satellites were used by Israel or the Arab states for reconnaissance and the transport of nuclear weapons, then such a use might be considered or construed by the opposing state as an act of war. Also, satellites might be used to disrupt radar and radio communications systems; such intrusions and disruptions might provoke an affected state to retaliate with a nuclear strike.

A misinterpretation of the identity and intentions of submarines also might induce a state to launch a nuclear strike. Moreover, attention should be called to "administrative accidents," namely, decisions to stage a nuclear strike without authorization by the competent decision-making bodies. An Israeli or Syrian pilot even might, as a result of psychological tension, drop a nuclear bomb on enemy territory. We already have the example of two attacks on sacred Muslim shrines in Jerusalem by deranged individuals, one of whom was a member of the Israeli armed forces.

3. Multiplicity of Nuclear States and Nuclear Weapons: The Middle East as Compared with the United States and the Soviet Union

The doctrine of nuclear deterrence is not ideal for preventing war and securing peace in the world. This doctrine has heightened the nightmare of uncertainty and fear. Nuclear arsenals in the world have grown in size, sophistication, and destructiveness beyond any conceivable purpose. The possessors of nuclear weapons justify the existence of those weapons by the doctrine of deterrence. There is, however, a growing suspicion that one day nuclear weapons might no longer be considered as a means of deterrence. The balance of terror implies an arms race.

According to the theory of the need for a military nuclear balance to maintain mutual deterrence, the balance is upset if a party possesses more weapons of a certian type or improves existing systems. From this view, it follows that every armament measure adopted by one party must be met with countermeasures by the other party. Thus, the arms race will continue *ad infinitum* in a vicious spiral. It would seem that no equilibrium that is accepted by both parties can ever be achieved in this way.

The concept of the nuclear balance, referred to as a balance of terror, implies that each adversary seeks to ensure a certain margin of superiority for fear of being placed at a disadvantage. Thus, in practice, the temptation is easy and the danger is always there that the search for balance is converted into a search for superiority. Additionally, since balance, quantitatively and qualitatively, is impossible, or almost impossible to be precisely determined and established, adversaries would always seek to ensure a certain margin of superiority. Obviously, this sets off the arms race in a dangerous manner. Indeed, the security aspect of atomic weapons is different from the security aspect of conventional weapons.

The technical problems of intelligence and analysis are very complicated. Even the Super Powers have not yet reached satisfactory solutions. It is very difficult to distinguish between test rockets and those on an attack flight, and even between possible attack flights and certain natural phenomena. It is not only that small states are dissimilar to Super Powers in their ability to establish facilities for intelligence and analysis, but also their situation is incomparably more difficult: The time duration between the release of missiles and their landing is shorter; consequently, there is no effective system for detecting the release of missiles for attack.

Any mishap arising from technical or human failure, of course, would probably bring nuclear tragedy, and the guarantees against mishaps and errors are likely to be diminished as the proliferation of nuclear arms increases because small states cannot overcome the complex technical and administrative problems involved very easily. That is, a nuclear-armed state conducts continual surveillance to ascertain whether a threat has arisen which would make it necessary, according to its assessment, to use its nuclear arms. If it believes that it will become the target of a nuclear attack, it would not hesitate to employ its arms. If a state decides that it is a target of nuclear attack by a neighboring state, it has little time in order to gather the necessary information, analyze it, decide on its reaction and implement its decision.

Israel is surrounded with Arab foes because its military, political, and settlement activities against Arabs within its borders and without are not viewed as legitimate. Thus, one may presume that its neighbors would wish to halt its expansion or force it to a negotiated peace. Should this fact lead Israel to be prepared with any weapon which it could acquire or produce? Israel's qualitative superiority in conventional weapons gives it the choice of avoiding the acquisition of nuclear weapons.

What seems preferable for Israeli and for Arab security and existence: Nuclear-free Middle East or a Middle East where some states, including Israel, have nuclear military capability? It could be safely assumed that an Arab-Israeli war in which conventional weapons are used is obviously preferable over a Middle Eastern war where Israel and the Arabs employ nuclear weapons.

The nuclear problem in the Middle East is much more complicated than, say, that between the United States and the Soviet Union. One of the salient features of the system of the United Sates-Soviet relations is that there are two major sides to the nuclear dialogue or equation. These two Super Powers devote major thinking to their mutual problems. The nuclear weapons possessed by France, Britain and China are not of such volume, at least now, as to divert the attention of the two Super Powers from thinking mainly about their mutual nuclear problems. However, the number of states in the Middle East that could acquire nuclear weapons would make it very difficult, if not impossible, to achieve détente. Even if they could, the multiplicity of states would make it easy for détente to be disrupted. The larger the number of states with nuclear capability in the Middle East the more difficult it will become to locate the source of a nuclear attack. Thus, the promotion of confidence in relations between Arab states and Israel would appear essential. The spread of nuclear weapons in the Middle East reduces the reliability of nuclear deterrence systems. A state, desirous of provoking a nuclear confrontation between Israel and other Middle Eastern states, might use its nuclear weapons, without disclosing its identity, against one of those states leaving the impression that the nuclear strike was launched by another Middle Eastern state. The state under attack, if it still had the capability, would strike against the state which is perceived erroneously as the attacker.

The danger of a nuclear war brought about by a third party has been diagnosed in United States-Soviet relations. Such a war has been described as catalytic. That contingency envisaged that a state possessing nuclear weapons and antagonistic to both the United States and the Soviet Union might make an attempt to produce a nuclear confrontation by unleashing a nuclear rocket attack against one of the two. The Super Power under attack might assume that the blow originated in the other Super Power and would launch a nuclear counterstrike against its traditional adversary. Meanwhile, the state provoking this nuclear exchange would be playing the role of a spectator.

In the course of time it has become clear that this particular possibility, though theoretically conceivable, is in practice remote for several reasons. First, the United States and the Soviet Union possess sophisticated tracking equipment with which they can determine with relative ease the origin of rockets launched against them. Second, both states can quickly find out whether this explosion was caused by the second party or not. Third, since the United States and the Soviet Union know of the existence of this contingency, they would take it into account if one of them is attacked. By contrast, the nuclear situation in the Middle East would involve at least two states, one of which would likely be Israel. To this equation should also be added non-Arab states and, as mentioned above, Palestinian national organizations which may acquire a nuclear option.

If denuclearization of the Middle East is the only alternative to the possibility of an atomic tragedy, then it follows that there can be no real nuclear deterrence in that region. Mutual destruction could be total. In the light of the foregoing, the primary security interest, that of existence, dictates elimination of nuclear weapons in the Middle East and avoidance of the development and acquisition by any Middle Eastern state of such weapons.

4. Second-Strike Nuclear Balance of Deterrence

Of relevance here is the concept of second-strike nuclear balance of deterrence. This means that two rival states possess nuclear weapons and that each of them is capable of absorbing a nuclear strike launched by its opponent and can retaliate with a nuclear strike of its own. One of the requirements for maintaining stable nuclear deterrence is to let it be known by the various countries that they possess a second-strike retaliatory capability. That is, stability depends on any potential attacker's being convinced that retaliation by an attacked state will inflict upon the attacker unacceptable damage.

The establishment of a nuclear second-strike capability requires mobility. The nuclear warheads should be kept in constant movement and they should be widely dispersed. Otherwise, they should be placed in underground silos and in places which make it difficult for other states to locate them. Spy satellites, however, now make concealment difficult to achieve. Of course, a large number of atomic devices should be deployed to diminish the likelihood that all the weapons would be destroyed in the attack. However, because of economic, technological and geographic considerations, states in the Middle East probably could not establish a second-strike capability. In the Middle East, whoever started a nuclear war would probably win it.

Second-strike capabilities, for example of the United States and the Soviet Union, are protected by placing sea-based missile forces in nuclear submarines the location of which is hidden from enemy intelligence by sea water in which detection impulses cannot pass over long distances, and by placing land-based intercontinental ballistic missiles (ICBM) in reinforced concrete silos which can withstand all but close hits.

One can advance the argument that conditions for the creation of second-strike deterrence cannot easily be secured in the Middle East; consequently, the establishment of a stable nuclear balance of terror is not feasible.[1] Under the prevailing circumstances in the Middle East the retaliatory, or second-strike, strategy at the core of the deterrent relationship between the United States and the Soviet Union cannot be applicable to the Middle East environment.

The atmosphere of deep suspicion prevailing between the Israelis and the Arabs places everyone under great tension and creates a major element of instability in the Middle East. As long as nuclear states have no second-strike capability they would always exist under the shadow of mutual fear and each of them might think that the other was planning a sudden nuclear strike against it. In such situations, deterrence might not be effective. A state might, therefore, be induced to move quickly, under circumstances of high tension, to employ its nuclear weapons first rather than be the target of a first strike. This scenario obviously increases the danger of a nuclear war.

Due to the geographical vastness of the Arab lands and the geographical smallness of Israel, the damage to Israel that could be produced by an Arab atomic attack would be much greater, from Israel's viewpoint, than that of an Israeli attack on Arab lands. Annihilation even by primitive atomic devices of Israel as a political, demographic and psychological entity would be easier than that of the Arab lands. If a number of Arab states launch a surprise nuclear attack on Israel it would be destroyed. In a situation where no Middle Eastern state has a nuclear second-strike capability, if Israel first dropped a number of atomic bombs on Arab countries it would subdue them. In each Arab country, there are several sites that are vital to that country's existence and that embrace its political, military, intellectual, industrial, business and technical elites. The destruction by nuclear missiles of these few targets would cripple such countries as viable demographic and socio-economic entities. However, some observers maintain that the emergence of a situation in which Israel and Arab states acquire nuclear weapons would ultimately be beneficial to the Arabs because such a situation would create an effective deterrent against Israel and would be instrumental in neutralizing Israel's nuclear capability; consequently, it would permit Arab conventional military power to score some military gains against the Israeli army, in view of the fact that Arab states would eventually enjoy a conventional capability larger than that of Israel.

5. Nuclear Deterrence: Is It Possible?

There are, perhaps, two ways in which stability might be achieved in the Middle East. One approach is political settlement, which involves territorial arrangements. The second approach assumes the permanence of the Israeli-Arab conflict, under which condition the various states strive to achieve stability through a stable balance of power. However, some scholars are of the view that, in practice, such a balance has meant that Israel has been required to achieve and maintain military superiority to deter Arab states from making attempts to regain their own territories.[2]

So far, the concept of military balance has failed in the Middle East because Israel has been able to become a military giant. As a matter of fact, some observers question the possibility of creating a stable military balance between Israel and the Arab states. In spite of Israel's military victories, in fact because of them, a number of Arab leaders and political thinkers have not abandoned the idea that the Arabs require a military capability to deter Israel. Some Israelis and non-Israelis explain this conduct as a sort of Arab irrationality, while ignoring the enormous acquisitions Israel has made when the Arabs have had a weak military posture.

The failure of the concept of conventional military balance is attributable to two factors: Arab expectations of qualitative and quantitative military improvements that would change the military balance in the Arab favor, and Arab awareness that military defeats have often meant diplomatic victories.

Unless we accept an assumption of a racial theory of Arab inferiority, the military victories that three million Israelis have inflicted on tens of millions of Arabs should be considered as unnatural occurrences that find their explanation in special circumstances. The author categorically rejects such a racial theory of inferiority and maintains that Israel's military victories resulted from various historical, social, political, economic, cultural and psychological variables in the Middle East and elsewhere, and particularly because the Israeli elite are Europeans.

Some experts in Middle Eastern politics advance explanations of the unnatural Israeli victories over the Arabs. In 1956, the 'special condition' was the French and British invasion of Egypt and the lack of Egyptian experience in the employment of modern arms. The special condition' in June 1967 was Israel's launching of a surprise attack on the Egyptian airfields, poor military command and lack of coordination among Arab armies. 'Special conditions' are also not lacking in the case of the 1948-49, 1973 and 1982 wars. That is, at present, for various historical reasons stemming from the absence of scientific knowledge and technological know-how in the Middle East, Israel enjoys technological superiority which has been decisive in its wars against Arab states. One can assume that if Arab states reduce and bridge the technological gap between them and Israel, then these states will be able to challenge Israel successfully.

The Arabs also realize they might suffer defeat in war but they can win at the negotiating table, for the United States, the Soviet Union and other big powers cannot tolerate, for economic and political reasons, the consequences of a complete defeat of the Arab states.

Rosen is of the view that the major objective of atomic weapons is deterrence, not fighting wars, and that the relevant question for Israel is whether it can threaten its Arab antagonists with damage that they too will consider unacceptable. He gave an affirmative answer to this question. He maintains that because of geographical and demographical realities in the Middle East, Israel can threaten its opponents with levels of damage that they will find unacceptable. The Israeli airforce has enjoyed decisive superiority over Arab airforces and can penetrate Arab airspace and strike in depth most Arab targets. Rosen noted that should Arab surface-to-air missile defenses challenge Israel's airforce superiority, as they did in the 1973 war, its locally manufactured offensive missiles (like Jericho with a striking range of 280 and 300 miles) can hit major cities in the Arab world from launching sites behind the pre-1967 borders of Israel. Rosen believes that a nuclear-armed

Israeli strike force would be sufficient to deter and destroy any Arab opponent who would attack with nuclear or massive conventional forces across Israel's borders.[3]

Rosen holds the view that a stable deterrence system of mutual assured destruction (MAD) is not ruled out by the problem of limited territory in a situation where two nuclear armed adversaries exist with delivery systems capable of penetrating enemy lines and of causing unacceptable levels of damage.[4]

This case for a policy of nuclear deterrence has been set forth by Fuad Jabber:

Where conventional power has failed, weapons of mass destruction would be expected to succeed in convincing Arab populations first and their governments second of the futility of continuing their confrontation with Israel. With the realization that Israel cannot be militarily defeated, the rationale behind the permanent state of war, the economic blockade, and the policy of non-acceptance and non-recognition might be expected to break down. Moreover, whatever tendencies towards recognition and negotiations may already exist in the Arab world would be enormously strengthened. Hitherto, governments willing to negotiate had not dared to act because their position at home would have become untenable. In a nuclear context, the survival imperative might provide enough justification to make such approaches possible... The psychologically erosive effects of the nuclear logic would be at work on the Arab will, gradually producing that pervasive feeling of 'doubt—and eventually resignation and despair—about the dream of eliminating Israel from the world's map,' that Israel's doctrine of deterrence had always sought to create.[5]

Jabber has not been the only writer in the Arab world who maintained that Israel's acquisition of nuclear weapons would be instrumental in guaranteeing the eventual security of Israel in the Middle East context. Ahmad Samih Khalidi, in his article entitled "An Appraisal of the Arab-Israeli Military Balance," wrote that when Israel acquires nuclear weapons, there would be a 'stalemate.' When Egypt acquires nuclear weapons "... neither country will dare attack the other... " and "... the sands will have run out for the Arabs."[6]

If Israel and certain Arab states possess nuclear capability, and if a nuclear balance prevails between them, then there would be a higher likelihood that military confrontations, if they take place, would be conducted with conventional arms which would lessen the danger of nuclear confrontations. The nuclear balance between the United States and the Soviet Union is founded on the second-strike nuclear balance of deterrence. What makes nuclear relations between the Super Powers less unstable, though not ideal, is the ability of one of the two to absorb a nuclear strike of some magnitude and then to retaliate with a nuclear blow of enormous power. These two powers have aircraft continuously flying, carrying nuclear rockets. Both have submarines equipped with nuclear rockets which are not easy to track and hit. They also have rockets placed in silos which are well protected against nuclear strikes.

It is correct to say that the expectations that govern mutual nuclear deterrence relations between the United States and the Soviet Union are much more structured than those which would govern mutual nuclear deterrence between Israelis and Arabs, if such deterrence would emerge. Before these two Super Powers attained a relatively stable balance of mutual deterrence in their nuclear relations there was a time (lasting until the middle of the 1960s) in which each of the two sides was concerned about the possibility that the opponent might launch a surprise nuclear strike which probably would have eliminated its nuclear force.

A nuclear balance of deterrence is not absolutely stable, because of the incessant developments in nuclear technology. Since the nuclear balance of deterrence is not absolute, the two Super Powers show a concern with the stability of this balance and they resort to various mechanisms such as agreements in order to preserve the balance. This pattern of relations is one of the major reasons why a nuclear war between them has been avoided. Also the sense of deep grievance observable in the Middle East is absent. Neither the United States nor the Soviet Union want to annihilate each other. This is also true in relation to some other states such as India and Pakistan, and the Soviet Union and France. It is more difficult to annihilate with one nuclear strike large and populous countries such as the Soviet Union, India, China, or the United States.

There are other differences between conditions of a Middle East possessing nuclear arms and conditions characterizing Soviet-American relations. Big powers, it may be argued, have a more realistic appreciation and knowledge of the difficulty of geographically limiting nuclear conflict than small states. Unlike many small states, the great powers have technological and military means of analysis which provide a more realistic evaluation of the situation. Moreover, the self-interest of the great powers is more identified with world interest than that of individual small states.

Middle Eastern states can of course learn much from United States' and Soviet rules of behavior concerning the avoidance of activating nuclear weapons. But, anxiety and tension in the Middle East, especially after Israel's activities in the nuclear field, have very much increased and the Middle East will doubtless continue to live in this way for a number of years until the nuclear states of the Middle East adopt patterns of conduct necessitated by nuclear reality.

To have a stable nuclear deterrence, it is not enough to have a nuclear technical balance. There should also exist a psychological balance. Even if Israel and Arab states reached stable nuclear deterrence, they would have to be willing to satisfy psychological requirements as well. The deep hatred and enmity between Israelis and Arabs and the deep sense of injustice felt by the Arabs must be overcome somehow, for the psychological and emotional makeup of some groups in the Middle East increases the likelihood of a crisis developing into a nuclear war. Territorial issues must be resolved. William B. Bader has argued that Israel's area before the June 1967 war did not encourage the Israelis to develop a nuclear force.[7] Before that war, during which Israel occupied the West Bank of the Jordan River, the Syrian Golan Heights overlooking the northeastern part of Israel, the Gaza Strip, and the Sinai Peninsula, Israel's tight inner lines of communication and supply were the major element in its defensive and offensive military operations. And before that war, Israel could move supplies and soldiers from one front to another in a matter of a few hours. Operating from these inner lines of communications and supplies in this relatively small area, Israel's military strategy was based on the use of a preemptive *Blitzkrieg* with conventional weapons. With its occupation of Arab territories, Israel's military policy underwent some change. Bader pointed out that "Israel, in order to offset the new problem of maintaining inner lines of communication and supply, may feel compelled to alter the mix of her defense strategy by taking up her option on nuclear weapons."[8]

Because of the short distances between strategic targets, delivery of nuclear weapons is relatively simple, surer, and more precise, and many Arab and Israeli targets are within the range of existing aircraft and rockets. Since Israeli and Arab air defenses are relatively easily penetrable, warplanes could, without missiles, be used in nuclear weapon delivery against the other side.

With respect to the introduction of nuclear weapons into the Middle East, the states of the area have another physical disincentive. They, especially Israel and Egypt, have a high population density in relatively small areas of land. Despite Egypt's size, which is 386,198 square miles, including Sinai, the Egyptian population and industry are highly concentrated along the Nile and in the upper third of the country, in Alexandria, Cairo and the towns along the Nile Delta. Egypt's vast empty expanses are ideal for the wide dispersion of missiles. Nevertheless, Egypt cannot absorb a nuclear attack on its two major cities of Alexandria and Cairo. The dropping of two small-sized or medium-sized nuclear bombs on these two cities would play havoc with Egypt's urban population and industrial capacity. If the Aswan Dam in Egypt were struck, then the whole Nile Valley would be flooded and perhaps millions of people would lose their lives.

Moreover, a third of Syria's population live in Latakia, Hama, Homs, Aleppo and Damascus. The population of Israel is also highly concentrated. All major cities are within easy striking range of bombers taking off from airfields in Jordan, Syria, Egypt, Saudi Arabia and Iraq. If these fighter bombers could be prevented by Israeli defenses from penetration, some Arab surface-to-surface missiles, like the Scud (with a range of 160-180 miles) could reach vital Israeli targets from these states. These arguments show that it would be even more unacceptable for Israel to enter a nuclear war than for a larger state to do so.

In spite of Israel's partially successful attempts to disperse its industrial plants and population, it is still highly vulnerable. Israel's size is relatively small; its closely packed population is concentrated within the Jerusalem, Haifa and Tel Aviv triangle and especially in a narrow and short coastal strip of land, with a length of nearly 120 miles stretching from the Lebanese border in the north to the Gaza Strip in the south, where the greater part of the population and industry is located. Israel could not survive a nuclear attack on this strip. Small nuclear bombs, of say the 19-kiloton type, would represent a very significant threat in a Middle Eastern context.

As far as the Arabs are concerned, Israel has defeated Arab states several times, and according to Arab mentality, the shame of defeat should be redressed.[9] This concern and other feelings of the Arabs and the Israelis towards each other are detrimental to the achievement of reasonable, stable nuclear deterrence. That is, some Israelis believe that since Israel has shown a number of times that it is stronger than the Arabs, the only rational step for the Arabs is to reach peace with Israel. But Arab political behavior will not necessarily be governed by this type of thinking. Arabs want a just solution. Israeli military victories might not convince Arab states that they should make peace with Israel if the terms are harsh or humiliating. Thus, Israeli political or military action, which is probably predicated on a misconception of the Arab mentality, might trigger an Arab reaction, unexpected by the Israelis, even leading some general staffs to resort to the use of atomic weapons. That is, in a situation where Israel and some Arab states have nuclear weapons, it would be probable that rational, reasoned calculation, dictated by the comprehension and magnitude of a nuclear threat to essential national interests, would give way to strong social, economic, political, and religious values. The prospect of resorting to the use of nuclear weapons is higher in states whose leaders are less sophisticated, more temperamental and emotional and whose conduct sometimes tends to be irrational. Obviously, it would be a tragedy if a state possessing nuclear weapons in the Middle East were to have such a leader.

At the very least, it is hoped that if both Israel and the Arab states come to possess nuclear weapons and a nuclear balance prevails between them, they would evolve only into a cold war relationship which would be waged in terms of diplomacy, economics, politics and a struggle for world public opinion.

FOOTNOTES

1. Y. Nimrod and A. Korczyn, "Suggested Patterns for Israeli-Egyptian Agreement to Avoid Nuclear Proliferation," *New Outlook*, January 1967, p. 9; E. Rutherford, "Israel and the Bomb," *Cambridge Review*, December 2, 1967, pp. 157-60.
2. Steven J. Rosen, "Nuclearization and Stability in the Middle East," in Onkar Marwah and Ann Schulz, eds., *Nuclear Proliferation and the Near-Nuclear Countries* (Cambridge, Mass.: Ballinger, 1975), p. 158.
3. *Ibid.*, pp. 163-64.
4. *Ibid.*

5. Fuad Jabber, *Israel and Nuclear Weapons: Present Option and Future Strategies* (London: Chatto and Windus for The International Institute for Strategic Studies, 1971), pp. 146-47.
6. Ahmad Samih Khalidi, "An Appraisal of the Arab-Israeli Military Balance," *Middle East Forum*, 42, 3, 1966, pp. 55, 63.
7. William B. Bader, *The United States and the Spread of Nuclear Weapons* (New York: Pegasus, 1968), p. 90.
8. *Ibid.*, p. 91.
9. Ciro E. Zoppo, "The Nuclear Genie in the Middle East," *New Outlook*, Vol. 18, No. 2 (157), February, 1975, p. 25.

FOURTEEN
UNITED NATIONS DOCUMENTS
RELATING TO THE
PROLIFERATION OF
NUCLEAR DEVICES IN THE
MIDDLE EAST,
SOUTH ASIA AND AFRICA

Document No. I

A Programme for Peace and International Cooperation

Members and Observers Present

The Second Conference of Heads of State or Government of the following non-aligned countries:

Afghanistan, Algeria, Angola, Burma, Burundi, Cambodia, Cameroon, Central African Republic, Ceylon, Chad, Congo (Brazzaville), Cuba, Cyprus, Dahomey, Ethiopia, Ghana, Guinea, India, Indonesia, Iraq, Islamic Republic of Mauritania, Jordan, Kenya, Kuwait, Laos, Lebanon, Liberia, Libya, Malawi, Mali, Morocco, Nepal, Nigeria, Saudi Arabia, Senegal, Sierra Leone, Somalia, Sudan, Syria, Togo, Tunisia, Uganda, United Arab Republic, United Republic of Tanganyika and Zanzibar, Yemen, Yugoslavia and Zambia was held in Cairo from 5 October to 10 October 1964.

The following countries: Argentine, Bolivia, Brazil, Chile, Finland, Jamaica, Mexico, Trinidad and Tobago, Uruguay and Venezuela were represented by observers.

The Secretary-General of the Organization of African Unity and the Secretary-General of the League of Arab States were present as observers.

* * *

The Heads of State or Government. . . express their agreement upon the following points:

General and Complete Disarmament; Peaceful Use of Atomic Energy, Prohibition of All Nuclear Weapon Tests, Establishment of Nuclear-Free Zones, Prevention of Dissemination of Nuclear Weapons and Abolition of All Nuclear Weapons

The Conference emphasises the paramount importance of disarmament as one of the basic problems of the contemporary world, and stresses the necessity of reaching immediate and practical solutions which would free mankind from the danger of war and from a sense of insecurity.

The Conference notes with concern that the continuing arms race an the tremendous advances that have been made in the production of weapons of mass destruction and their stockpiling threaten the world with armed conflict and annihilation. The Conference urges the great Powers to take new and urgent steps towards achieving general and complete disarmament under strict and effective international control.

The Conference regrets that despite the efforts of the members of the 18-Nation Committee on Disarmament, and in particular those of the non-aligned countries, the results have not been satisfactory. It urges the Great Powers, in collaboration with the other members of that Committee, to renew their efforts with determination with a view to the rapid conclusion of an agreement on general and complete disarmament.

The Conference calls upon all States to accede to the Moscow treaty partially banning the testing of nuclear weapons, and to abide by its provisions in the interests of peace and the welfare of humanity.

The Conference urges the extension of the Moscow Treaty so as to include underground tests, and the discontinuance of such tests pending the extension of the agreement.

The Conference appeals to the Great Powers to take the lead in giving effect to decisive and immediate measures which would make possible substantial reductions in their military budgets.

The Conference requests the Great Powers to abstain from all policies conducive to the dissemination of nuclear weapons and their by-products among those States which do not at present possess them. It underlines the great danger in the dissemination of nuclear weapons and urges all States, particularly those possessing nuclear weapons, to conclude non-dissemination agreements and to agree on measures providing for the gradual liquidation of the existing stock-piles of nuclear weapons.

The Conference welcomes the agreement of the Great Powers not to orbit in outer space nuclear or other weapons of mass destruction and expresses its conviction that it is necessary to conclude an international treaty prohibiting the utilisation of outer space for military purposes. The Conference urges full international cooperation in the peaceful uses of outer space.

The Conference considers that the declaration by African States regarding the denuclearization of Africa, the aspirations of the Latin American countries to denuclearize their continent and the various proposals pertaining to the denuclearization of areas in Europe and Asia are steps in the right direction because they assist in consolidating international peace and security and lessening international tensions.

The Conference recommends the establishment of denuclearized zones covering these and other areas and the oceans of the world, particularly those which have been hitherto free from nuclear weapons, in accordance with the desires expressed by the States and peoples concerned.

The Conference urges all nations to join in the cooperative development of the peaceful use of atomic energy for the benefit of all mankind; and in particular, to study the development of atomic power and other technical aspects in which international cooperation might be most effectively accomplished through the free flow of such scientific information.

Document No. II

United Nations General Assembly Official Records

Annexes Twentieth Session
New York, 1965

Agenda Item 105: Declaration on the Denuclearization of Africa

Letter dated 14 September 1965 from the Permanent Representatives of Algeria, Burundi, Cameroon, the Central African Republic, Chad, the Congo (Brazzaville), Dahomey, Ethiopia, Gabon, Ghana, Guinea, the Ivory Coast, Kenya, Liberia, Libya, Madagascar, Malawi, Mali, Mauritania, Morocco, Niger, Nigeria, Rwanda, Senegal, Sierra Leone, Somalia, the Sudan, Togo, Tunisia, Uganda, the United Arab Republic, the United Republic of Tanzania, the Upper Volta and Zambia to the United Nations addressed to the Secretary-General.

The undersigned Permanent Representatives of the African States have the honour to draw to your attention the declaration on the denuclearization of Africa adopted by the Assembly of Heads of State and Government of the Organization of African Unity at its first regular session, held at Cairo from 17 to 21 July 1964, which reads as follows:

"*We, African Heads of State and Government,*

Conscious of our responsibilities towards our peoples and of our international obligation, under the Charter of the United Nations and the Charter of the Organization of African Unity, to use our best endeavours to strengthen peace and security,

Convinced that the conditions ensuring international peace and security must prevail in order to save humanity from the scourge of nuclear war,

Profoundly concerned at the effects of the dissemination of nuclear weapons,

Confirming resolution 1652 (XVI) of the United Nations General Assembly, calling upon all States to respect the denuclearization of the continent of Africa,

Reaffirming the resolution on general disarmament adopted by the Conference of Heads of State and Government at Addis Ababa in May 1963,

Conscious that the General Assembly of the United Nations, at its sixteenth session, called upon all States, and in particular upon the States at present possessing nuclear weapons, to use their best endeavours to secure the conclusion of an international agreement containing provisions under which the nuclear States would undertake to refrain from relinquishing control of nuclear weapons and from transmitting the information necessary for their manufacture to States not possessing such weapons and provisions under which States not possessing nuclear weapons would undertake not to manufacture or otherwise acquire control of such weapons,

Convinced of the urgent necessity to redouble the efforts to reach an early solution to the problem of general disarmament,

"1. *Solemnly declare* that we are ready to undertake, through an international agreement to be concluded under United Nations auspices, not to manufacture or control atomic weapons;

"2. *Appeal* to all peace-loving nations to accept the same undertaking;

"3. *Appeal* to all the nuclear Powers to respect this declaration and conform to it;

"4. *Request* the General Assembly of the United Nations, at its nineteenth regular session, to approve this declaration and to take the necessary measures to convene an international conference for the purpose of concluding an agreement to that effect."

Document No. III

A Resolution of the United Nations General Assembly (22nd Session, 1672 Plenary Meeting, 12 June, 1968)

Treaty on the Non-Proliferation of Nuclear Weapons

The States concluding this Treaty, hereinafter referrred to as the "Parties to the Treaty,"

Considering the devastation that would be visited upon all mankind by a nuclear war and the consequent need to make every effort to avert the danger of such a war and to take measures to safeguard the security of peoples,

Believing that the proliferation of nuclear weapons would seriously enhance the danger of nuclear war,

In conformity with resolutions of the United Nations General Assembly calling for the conclusion of an agreement on the prevention of wider dissemination of nuclear weapons,

Undertaking to co-operate in facilitating the application of International Atomic Energy Agency safequards on peaceful nuclear activities,

Expressing their support for research, development and other efforts to further the application, within the framework of the International Atomic Energy Agency safeguards system, of the principle of safeguarding effectively the flow of source and special fissionable materials by use of instruments and other techniques at certain strategic points,

Affirming the principle that the benefits of peaceful applications of nuclear technology, including any technological by-products which may be derived by nuclear-weapon States from the development of nuclear explosive devices, should be available for peaceful purposes to all Parties to the Treaty, whether nuclear-weapon or non-nuclear-weapon States,

Convinced that, in furtherance of this principle, all Parties to the Treaty are entitled to participate in the fullest possible exchange of scientific information for, and to contribute alone or in co-operation with other States to, the further development of the applications of atomic energy for peaceful purposes,

Declaring their intention to achieve at the earliest possible date the cessation of the nuclear arms race and to undertake effective measures in the direction of nuclear disarmament,

Urging the co-operation of all States in the attainment of this objective,

Recalling the determination expressed by the Parties to the 1963 Treaty banning nuclear weapon tests in the atmosphere, in outer space and under water in its Preamble to seek to achieve the discontinuance of all test explosions to nuclear weapons for all time and to continue negotiations to this end,

Desiring to further the easing of international tension and the strengthening of trust between States in order to facilitate the cessation of the manufacture of nuclear weapons, the liquidation of all their existing stockpiles, and the elimination from national arsenals of nuclear weapons and the means of their delivery pursuant to a treaty on general and complete disarmament under strict and effective international control,

Recallling that, in accordance with the Charter of the United Nations, States must refrain in their international relations from the threat or use of force against the territorial integrity or political independence of any State, or in any other manner inconsistent with the Purposes of the United Nations, and that the establishment and maintenance of international peace and security are to be promoted with the least diversion for armaments of the world's human and economic resources,

Have agreed as follows:

ARTICLE I

Each nuclear-weapon State Party to the Treaty undertakes not to transfer to any recipient whatsoever nuclear weapons or other nuclear explosive devices or control over such weapons or explosive devices directly, or indirectly; and not in any way to assist, encourage or induce any non-nuclear-weapon State to manufacture or otherwise acquire nuclear weapons or other nuclear explosive devices, or control over such weapons or explosive devices.

ARTICLE II

Each non-nuclear-weapon State Party to the Treaty undertakes not to receive the transfer from any transferor whatsoever of nuclear weapons or other nuclear explosive devices or of control over such weapons or explosive devices directly, or indirectly; not to manufacture or otherwise acquire nuclear weaponas or other nuclear explosive devices; and not to seek or receive any assistance in the manufacture of nuclear weapons or other nuclear explosive devices.

ARTICLE III

1. Each non-nuclear-weapon State Party to the Treaty undertakes to accept safeguards, as set forth in an agreement to be negotiated and concluded with the International Atomic Energy Agency in accordance with the Statute of the International Atomic Energy Agency and the Agency's safeguards system, for the exclusive purpose of verification of the fulfillment of its obligations assumed under this Treaty with a view to preventing diversion of nuclear energy from peaceful uses to nuclear weapons or other nuclear explosive devices. Procedures for the safeguards required by this article shall be followed with respect to source or special fissionable material whether it is being produced, processed or used in any principal nuclear facility or is outside any such facility. The safeguards required by this article shall be applied on all source or special fissionable material in all peaceful nuclear activities within the territory of such State, under its jurisdiction, or carried out under its control anywhere.

2. Each State Party to the Treaty undertakes not to provide: *(a)* source or special fissionable material, or *(b)* equipment or material especially designed or prepared for the processing, use or production of special fissionable material, to any non-nuclear-weapon State for peaceful purposes, unless the source or special fissionable material shall be subject to the safeguards required by this article.

3. The safeguards required by this article shall be implemented in a manner designed to comply with article IV of this Treaty, and to avoid hampering the economic or technological development of the Parties or international cooperation in the field of peaceful nuclear activities, including the international exchange of nuclear material and equipment for the processing, use or produc-

tion of nuclear material for peaceful purposes in accordance with the provisions of this article and the principle of safeguarding set forth in the Preamble of the Treaty.

4. Non-nuclear-weapon States Party to the Treaty shall conclude agreements with the International Atomic Energy Agency to meet the requirements of this article either individually or together with other States in accordance with the Statute of the International Atomic Energy Agency. Negotiation of such agreements shall commence within 180 days from the original entry into force of this Treaty. For States depositing their instruments of ratification or accession after the 180-day period, negotiation of such agreements shall commence not later than the date of such deposit. Such agreements shall enter into force not later than eighteen months after the date of initiation of negotiations.

ARTICLE IV

1. Nothing in this Treaty shall be interpreted as affecting the inalienable right of all the Parties to the Treaty to develop research, production and use of nuclear energy for peaceful purposes without discrimination and in conformity with articles I and II of this Treaty.

2. All the Parties to the Treaty undertake to facilitate, and have the right to participate in, the fullest possible exchange of equipment, materials and scientific and technological information for the peaceful uses of nuclear energy. Parties to the Treaty in a position to do so shall also co-operate in contributing alone or together with other States or international organizations to the further development of the applications of nuclear energy for peaceful purposes, especially in the territories of non-nuclear-weapon States Party to the Treaty, with due consideration for the needs of the developing areas of the world.

ARTICLE V

Each Party to the Treaty undertakes to take appropriate measures to ensure that, in accordance with this Treaty, under appropriate international observation and through appropriate international procedures, potential benefits from any peaceful applications of nuclear explosions will be made available to non-nuclear-weapon States Party to the Treaty on a non-discriminatory basis and that the charge to such Parties for the explosive devices used will be as low as possible and exclude any charge for research and development. Non-nuclear-weapon States Party to the Treaty shall be able to obtain such benefits, pursuant to a special international agreement or agreements, through an appropriate international body with adequate representation of non-nuclear-weapon States. Negotiations on this subject shall commence as soon as possible after the Treaty enters into force. Non-nuclear-weapon States Party to the Treaty so desiring may also obtain such benefits pursuant to bilateral agreements.

ARTICLE VI

Each of the Parties to the Treaty undertakes to pursue negotiations in good faith on effective measures relating to cessation of the nuclear arms race at an early date and to nuclear disarmament, and on a treaty on general and complete disarmament under strict and effective international control.

ARTICLE VII

Nothing in this Treaty affects the right of any group of States to conclude regional treaties in order to assure the total absence of nuclear weapons in their respective territories.

* * *

ARTICLE IX

1. This Treaty shall be open to all States for signature. Any State which does not sign the Treaty before its entry into force in accordance with paragraph 3 of this article may accede to it at any time.

2. This Treaty shall be subject to ratification by signatory States. Instruments of ratification and instruments of accession shall be deposited with the Governments of the Union of Soviet Socialist Republics, the United Kingdom of Great Britain and Northern Ireland and the United States of America, which are hereby designated the Depositary Governments.

3. This Treaty shall enter into force after its ratification by the States, the Governments of which are designated Depositaries of the Treaty, and forty other States signatory to this Treaty and the

deposit of their instruments of ratification. For the purposes of this Treaty, a nuclear-weapon States is one which has manufactured and exploded a nuclear weapoon or other nuclear explosive device prior to 1 January 1967.

4. For States whose instruments of ratification or accession are deposited subsequent to the entry into force of this Treaty, it shall enter into force on the date of the deposit of their instruments of ratification or accession.

* * *

ARTICLE X

1. Each Party shall in exercising its national sovereignty have the right to withdraw from the Treaty if it decides that extraordinary events, related to the subject-matter of this Treaty, have jeopardized the supreme interests of its country. It shall give notice of such withdrawal to all other Parties to the Treaty and to the United Nations Security Council three months in advance. Such notice shall include a statement of the extraordinary events it regards as having jeopardized its supreme interests.

2. Twenty-five years after the entry into force of the Treaty, a conference shall be convened to decide whether the Treaty shall continue in force indefinitely, or shall be extended for an additional fixed period or periods. This decision shall be taken by a majority of the Parties to the Treaty.

* * *

Document No. IV

A Resolution of the United Nations General Assembly (29th Session, 9 December, 1974)

Establishment of a Nuclear-Weapon-Free Zone in the Region of the Middle East

The General Assembly,

Having considered the question of the establishment of a nuclear-weapon-free zone in the region of the Middle East,

Desiring to contribute to the maintenance of international peace and security by bolstering and expanding the existing regional and global structures for the prohibition and/or prevention of the further spread of nuclear weapons,

Realizing that the establishment of nuclear-weapon-free zones with an adequate system of safeguards could accelerate the process towards nuclear disarmament and the ultimate goal of general and complete disarmament under effective international control,

Recalling the resolution adopted by the Council of the League of Arab States at its sixty-second session, held in Cairo from 1 to 4 September 1974, on this subject,

Recalling the message sent by His Imperial Majesty the Shahanshah of Iran on 16 September 1974 on the establishment of a nuclear-weapon-free zone in the region of the Middle East,

Considering that the establishment of nuclear-weapon-free zones, on the initiative of the States situated within each zone concerned, is one of the measures which can contribute most effectively to halting the proliferation of those instruments of mass destruction and to promoting progress towards nuclear disarmament, with the goal of total destruction of all nuclear weapons and their means of delivery,

Mindful of the political conditions particular to the region of the Middle East and of the potential danger emanating therefrom, which would be further aggravated by the introduction of nuclear weapons in the area,

Conscious, therefore, of the need to keep the countries of the region from becoming involved in a ruinous nuclear arms race,

Recalling the Declaration on the Denuclearization of Africa issued by the Assembly of Heads of State and Government of the Organization of African Unity in July 1964,

Noting that the establishment of a nuclear-weapon-free zone in the region of the Middle East would contribute effectively to the realization of aims enunciated in the Declaration on the Denuclearization of Africa,

Recalling the notable achievement of the countries of Latin America in establishing a nuclear-free zone,

Also recalling resolution B of the Conference of Non-Nuclear-Weapon States held in Geneva from 29 August to 28 September 1968, in which the Conference recommended that non-nuclear-weapon States not comprised in the Latin American nuclear-free zone should study the possibility and desirability of establishing military denuclearization of their respective zones,

Recalling the aims pursued by the Treaty on the Non-Proliferation of Nuclear Weapons, in particular the goal of preventing the further spread of nuclear weapons,

Recalling its resolution 2373 (XXII) of 12 June 1968, in which it expressed the hope for the widest possible adherence to the Treaty on the Non-Proliferation of Nuclear Weapons by both nuclear-weapon and non-nuclear-weapon States,

1. *Commends* the idea of the establishment of a nuclear-weapon-free zone in the region of the Middle East;

2. *Considers* that, in order to advance the idea of a nuclear-weapon-free zone in the region of the Middle East, it is indispensable that all parties concerned in the area proclaim solemnly and immediately their intention to refrain , on a reciprocal basis, from producing, testing, obtaining, acquiring or in any other way possessing nuclear weapons;

3. *Calls upon* the parties concerned in the area to accede to the Treaty on the Non-Proliferation of Nuclear Weapons;

4. *Expresses the hope* that all States, in particular the nuclear-weapon States, will lend their full co-operation for the effective realization of the aims of the present resolution;

5. *Requests* the Secretary-General to ascertain the views of the parties concerned with respect to the implementation of the present resolution, in particular with regard to its paragraphs 2 and 3, and to report to the Security Council at an early date and, subsequently, to the General Assembly at its thirtieth session;

5. *Decides* to include in the provisional agenda of its thirtieth session the item entitled "Establishment of a nuclear-weapon-free zone in the region of the Middle East."

2309th plenary meeting

Document No. V

A Resolution of the United Nations General Assembly (31st Session, 10 December 1976)

Establishment of a Nuclear-Weapon-Free Zone in the Region of the Middle East

The General Assembly,

Recalling its resolution 3263 (XXIX) of 9 December 1974, in which it overwhelmingly commended the idea of the establishment of a nuclear-weapon-free zone in the region of the Middle East,

Recalling also its resolution 3474 (XXX) of 11 December 1975, in which it recognized that the establishment of a nuclear-weapon-free zone in the Middle East enjoys wide support in the region,

Mindful of the prevailing political situation in the region and the potential danger emanating therefrom that would be further aggravated by the introduction of nuclear weapons in the area,

Concerned that the lack of any appreciable progress in the direction of the establishment of a nuclear-weapon-free zone, in the present atmosphere in the region, will further complicate the situation,

Convinced that progress towards the establishment of a nuclear-weapon-free zone in the Middle East will greatly enhance the cause of peace both in the region and in the world,

Conscious of the particular nature of the problems involved and the complexities inherent in the situation in the Middle East, and the urgency of keeping the region free from involvement in a ruinous nuclear-arms race,

1. *Expresses the need* for further action to generate momentum towards realization of the establishment of a nuclear-weapon-free zone in the Middle East;

2. *Urges* all parties directly concerned to adhere to the Treaty on the Non-Proliferation of Nuclear Weapons as a means of promoting this objective;

3. *Reiterates* its recommendation that the Member States referred to in paragraph 2 above, pending the establishment of the

nuclear-weapon-free zone under an effective system of safeguards, should:

(a) Proclaim solemnly and immediately their intention to refrain, on a reciprocal basis, from producing, acquiring or in any other way possessing nuclear weapons and nuclear explosive devices and from permitting the stationing of nuclear weapons in their territory or the territory under their control by any third party;

(b) Refrain, on a reciprocal basis, from any other action that would facilitate the acquisition, testing or use of such weapons, or would be in any other way detrimental to the objective of the establishment of a nuclear-weapon-free zone in the region under an effective system of safeguards;

(c) Agree to place all their nuclear activities under the International Atomic Energy Agency safeguards;

4. *Reaffirms* the recommendations to the nuclear-weapon States to refrain from any action contrary to the purpose of the present resolution and the objective of establishing, in the region of the Middle East, a nuclear-weapon-free zone under an effective system of safeguards and to extend their co-operation ot the States of the region in their efforts to promote this objective;

5. *Invites* the Secretary-General to explore the possibilities of making progress towards the establishment of a nuclear-weapon-free zone in the area of the Middle East;

6. *Decides* to include in the provisional agenda of its thirty-second session the item entitled "Establishment of a nuclear-weapon-free zone in the region of the Middle East."

96th plenary meeting

Document No. VI

A Resolution of the United Nations General Assembly (32nd Session, 12 December 1977)

Establishment of a Nuclear-Weapon-Free Zone in the Region of the Middle East

The General Assembly,

Recalling its resolution 3263 (XXIX) of 9 December 1974, in which it overwhelmingly commended the idea of the establishment of a nuclear-weapon-free zone in the region of the Middle East,

Recalling also its resolution 3474 (XXX) of 11 December 1975, in which it recognized that the establishment of a nuclear-weapon-free zone in the Middle East enjoys wide support in the region,

Further recalling its resolution 31/71 of 10 December 1976, in which it expressed the conviction that progress towards the establishment of a nuclear-weapon-free zone in the Middle East would greatly enhance the cause of peace both in the region and in the world,

Mindful of the growing international desire for establishing a just and lasting peace in the region of the Middle East,

Conscious of the global apprehension over possible proliferation of nuclear weapons, in particular in the sensitive region of the Middle East,

Fully convinced that the possible development of nuclear capability would further complicate the situation and immensely damage the efforts to create an atmosphere of confidence in the Middle East,

Reiterating anew the particular nature of the problems involved and the complexities inherent in the situation in the Middle East, and the urgency of keeping the region free from involvement in a ruinous nuclear-arms race,

Recognizing, as a consequence, the need to create momentum towards the goal of establishing a nuclear-weapon-free zone in the Middle East,

1. *Urges anew* all parties directly concerned to adhere to the Treaty on the Non-Proliferation of Nuclear Weapons as a means of promoting this objective;

2. *Reiterates* its recommendation that the Member States referred to in paragraph 1 above, pending the establishment of a nuclear-weapon-free zone under an effective system of safeguards, should:

(a) Proclaim solemnly and immediately their intention to refrain, on a reciprocal basis, from producing, acquiring or in any other way possessing nuclear weapons and nuclear explosive devices and from permitting the stationing of nuclear weapons on their territory or the territory under their control by any third party;

(b) Refrain, on a reciprocal basis, from any other action that would facilitate the acquisition, testing or use of such weapons, or would be in any other way detrimental to the objective of the establishment of a nuclear-weapon-free zone in the region under an effective system of safeguards;

(c) Agree to place all their nuclear activities under the International Atomic Energy Agency safeguards;

3. *Reaffirms* its recommendation to the nuclear-weapon States to refrain from any action contrary to the purpose of the present resolution and the objective of establishing, in the region of the Middle East, a nuclear-weapon-free zone under an effective system of safeguards and to extend their co-operation to the States of the region in their efforts to promote this objective;

4. *Renews* its invitation to the Secretary-General to continue to explore the possiblities of making progress towards the establishment of a nuclear-weapon-free zone in the region of the Middle East;

5. *Decides* to include in the provisional agenda of its thirty-third session the item entitled "Establishment of a nuclear-weapon-free zone in the region of the Middle East."

100th plenary meeting

Document No. VII

A Resolution of the United Nations General Assembly (36th Session, 9 December 1981)

Establishment of a Nuclear-Weapon-Free Zone in the Region of the Middle East

A

The General Assembly,

Recalling its resolutions 3263 (XXIX) of 9 December 1974, 3474 (XXX) of 11 December 1975, 31/71 of 10 December 1976, 32/82 of 12 December 1977, 33/64 of 14 December 1978, 34/77 of 11 December 1979 and 35/147 of 12 December 1980 on the establishment of a nuclear-weapon-free zone in the region of the Middle East,

1. *Requests* the Secretary-General to transmit General Assembly resolution 35/147 to the Assembly at its second special session devoted to disarmament, to be held from 7 June to 9 July 1982;

2. *Decides* to include in the provisional agenda of its thirty-seventh session the item entitled "Establishment of a nuclear-weapon-free zone in the region of the Middle East."

91st plenary meeting

B

The General Assembly,

Recalling its resolutions concerning the establishment of a nuclear-weapon-free zone in the region of the Middle East,

Recalling also the recommendations for the establishment of such a zone in the Middle East consistent with paragraphs 60 to 63, in particular paragraph 63 *(d)*, of the Final Document of the Tenth Special Session of the General Assembly, the first special session devoted to disarmament,

Recalling further Security Council resolution 487 (1981) of 19 June 1981,

Taking into consideration the resolution adopted on 12 June 1981 by the Board of Governors of the International Atomic Energy Agency and resolution GC(XXV)/RES/ 381 adopted on 26 September 1981 by the General Conference of the Agency,

Recalling further the report of the Secretary-General concerning Israeli nuclear armament,

Realizing that adherence to the Treaty on the Non-Proliferation of Nuclear Weapons by all parties of the region will be conducive to a speedy establishment of a nuclear-weapon-free zone,

Deeply concerned that the future of the Treaty on the Non-Proliferation of Nuclear Weapons in the region has been gravely endangered by the attack carried out by Israel, which is not a party to the Treaty, on the nuclear installations of Iraq, which is a party to that Treaty,

1. *Considers* that the Israeli military attack on the Iraqi nuclear installations adversely affects the prospects of the establishment of a nuclear-weapon-free zone in the region of the Middle East;

2. *Declares* that it is imperative, in this respect, that Israel place forthwith all its nuclear facilities under International Atomic Energy Agency safeguards;

3. *Requests* the Secretary-General to transmit the present resolution to the General Assembly at its second special session devoted to disarmament.

91st plenary meeting

Document No. VIII

A Resolution of the United Nations General Assembly (26th Session, 16 December 1971)

Declaration of the Indian Ocean as a Zone of Peace

The General Assembly,

Conscious of the determination of the peoples of the littoral and hinterland States of the Indian Ocean to preserve their independence, sovereignty and territorial integrity, and to resolve their political, economic and social problems under conditions of peace and tranquility,

Recalling the Declaration of the Third Conference of Heads of State or Government of Non-Aligned Countries, held at Lusaka from 8 to 10 September 1970, calling upon all States to consider and respect the Indian Ocean as a zone of peace from which great Power rivalries and competition as well as bases conceived in the context of such rivalries and competition should be excluded, and declaring that the area should also be free of nuclear weapons,

Convinced of the desirability of ensuring the maintenance of such conditions in the Indian Ocean area by means other than military alliances, as such alliances entail financial and other obligations that call for the diversion of the limited resources of the States of the area from the mor compelling and productive task of economic and social reconstruction and could further involve them in the rivalries of power blocs in a manner prejudicial to their independence and freedom of action, thereby increasing international tensions,

Concerned at recent developments that portend the extension of the arms race into the Indian Ocean area, thereby posing a serious threat to the maintenance of such conditions in the area,

Convinced that the establishment of a zone of peace in the Indian Ocean would contribute towards arresting such developments, relaxing international tensions and strengthening international peace and security,

Convinced further that the establishment of a zone of peace in an extensive geographical area in one region could have a beneficial influence on the establishment of permanent universal peace based on equal rights and justice for all, in accordance with the purposes and principles of the Charter of the United Nations,

1. *Solemnly declares* that the Indian Ocean, within limits to be determined, together with the air space above and the ocean floor subjacent thereto, is hereby designated for all time as a zone of peace;

2. *Calls upon* the great Powers, in conformity with this Declaration, to enter into immediate consultations with the littoral States of the Indian Ocean with a view to:

(a) Halting the further escalation and expansion of their military presence in the Indian Ocean;

(b) Eliminating from the Indian Ocean all bases, military installations and logistical supply facilities, the disposition of nuclear weapons and weapons of mass destruction and any manifestation of great Power military presence in the Indian Ocean conceived in the context of great Power rivalry;

3. *Calls upon* the littoral and hinterland States of the Indian Ocean, the permanent members of the Security Council and other major maritime users of the Indian Ocean, in pursuit of the objective of establishing a system of universal collective security without military alliances and strengthening international security through regional and other co-operation, to enter into consultations with a view to the implementation of this Declaration and such action as may be necessary to ensure that:

(a) Warships and military aircraft may not use the Indian Ocean for any threat or use of force against the sovereignty, territorial integrity and independence of any littoral or hinterland State of the Indian Ocean in contravention of the purposes and principles of the Charter of the United Nations;

(b) Subject to the foregoing and to the norms and principles of international law, the right to free and unimpeded use of the zone by the vessels of all nations is unaffected;

(c) Appropriate arrangements are made to give effect to any international agreement that may ultimately be reached for the maintenance of the Indian Ocean as a zone of peace;

4. *Requests* the Secretary-General to report to the General Assembly at its twenty-seventh session on the progress that has been

made with regard to the implementation of this Declaration;

5. *Decides* to include in the provisional agenda of its twenty-seventh session an item entitled "Declaration of the Indian Ocean as a zone of peace."

2022nd plenary meeting

Document No. IX

A Resolution of the United Nations General Assembly (36th Session, 9 December 1981)

Israeli Nuclear Armament

The General Assembly,

Recalling its relevant resolutions on the establishment of a nuclear-weapon-free zone in the region of the Middle East,

Recalling also its resolutions 33/71 A of 14 December 1978 on military and nuclear collaboration with Israel and 34/89 of 11 December 1979 and 35/157 of 12 December 1980 on Israeli nuclear armament,

Alarmed by the increasing evidence regarding Israel's attempts to acquire nuclear weapons,

Noting with concern that Israel has persistently refused to adhere to the Treaty on the Non-Proliferation of Nuclear Weapons despite repeated calls by the General Assembly and the Security Council to place its nuclear facilities under International Atomic Energy Agency safeguards,

Recalling Security Council resolution 487 (1981) of 19 June 1981,

Recalling the resolution adopted on 12 June 1981 by the Board of Governors of the International Atomic Energy Agency and resolution GC(XXV)/RES/381 adopted on 26 September 1981 by the General Conference of the Agency, in which the Conference, *inter alia,* considered the Israeli act of aggression as an attack against the Agency and its safeguards régime and decided to suspend the provision of any assistance to Israel,

Recalling its repeated condemnation of the nuclear collaboration between Israel and South Africa,

Taking note of the report of the Secretary-General transmitting the study of the Group of Experts to Prepare a Study on Israeli Nuclear Armament,

1. *Expresses its appreciation* to the Secretary-General for his report on Israeli nuclear armament;

2. *Expresses its deep alarm* at the fact that the report has established that Israel has the technical capability to manufacture nuc-

lear weapons and possesses the means of delivery of such weapons;

3. *Also expresses its deep concern* that Israel has undermined the credibility of the International Atomic Energy Agency safeguards, in particular by the bombing of the Iraqi nuclear facilities which were under Agency safeguards;

4. *Reaffirms* that Israel's attack on the Iraqi nuclear facilities and Israel's capability constitute a serious destabilizng factor in an already tense situation in the Middle East, and a grave danger to international peace and security;

5. *Requests* the Security Council to prohibit all forms of cooperation with Israel in the nuclear field;

6. *Calls upon* all States and other parties and institutions to terminate forthwith all nuclear collaboration with Israel;

7. *Requests* the Security Council to institute effective enforcement action against Israel so as to prevent it from endangering international peace and security by its nuclear-weapon capability;

8. *Demands* that Israel should renounce, without delay, any possession of nuclear weapons and place all its nuclear activities under international safeguards;

9. *Requests* the Secretary-General to give maximum publicity to the report on Israeli nuclear armament and to distribute it to Member States, the specialized agencies and the Internaitonal Atomic Energy Agency and non-governmental organizations, so that the international community and public opinion may be fully aware of the danger inherent in Israel's nuclear capability;

10. *Also requests* the Secretary-General to follow closely Israeli military nuclear activity and to report thereon as appropriate;

11. *Further requests* the Secretary-General to transmit the report on Israeli nuclear armament to the General Assembly at its second special session devoted to disarmament;

12. *Decides* to include in the provisional agenda of its thirty-seventh session the item entitled "Israeli nuclear armament."

91st plenary meeting

Document No. X

A Resolution of the United Nations General Assembly (30th Session, 11 December 1975)

Implementation of the Declaration on the Denuclearization of Africa

The General Assembly,

Convinced that nuclear-weapon-free zones provide the best and easiest means whereby non-nuclear-weapon States can, by their own initiative and effort, ensure the total absence of nuclear weapons from their territories and enhance their mutual security,

Mindful of the fact that nuclear-weapon-free zones strengthen and promote the régime for the non-proliferation of nuclear weapons,

Reaffirming the inalienable right of all States to develop research, production and use of nuclear energy for peaceful purposes,

Recalling its resolutions 1652 (XVI) of 24 November 1961, 2033 (XX) of 3 December 1965 and 3261 E (XXIX) of 9 December 1974, which called upon all States to consider and respect the continent of Africa, including the continental African States, Madagascar and other islands surrounding Africa, as a nuclear-weapon-free zone,

Noting the solemn Declaration on the Denuclearization of Africa, adopted by the Assembly of Heads of State and Government of the Organization of African Unity at its first ordinary session, held at Cairo from 17 to 21 July 1964,

Noting also that the aforementioned Declaration was endorsed by the Second Conference of Heads of State or Government of Non-Aligned Countries, held at Cairo from 5 to 10 October 1964,

1. *Agrees* that implementation of the Declaration on the Denuclearization of Africa, adopted by the Assembly of Heads of State and Government of the Organization of African Unity, will be significant measure to prevent the proliferation of nuclear weapons in the world, conducive to general and complete disarmament, particularly nuclear disarmament;

2. *Reaffirms* its call upon all States to respect and abide by the Declaration on the Denuclearization of Africa;

3. *Reaffirms further* its call upon all States to consider and respect the continent of Africa, including the continental African States, Madagascar and other islands surrounding Africa, as a nuclear-weapon-free zone;

4. *Reiterates* its call upon all States to refrain from testing, manufacturing, deploying, transporting, storing, using or threatening to use nuclear weapons on the African continent;

5. *Requests* the Secretary-General to render all necessary assistance to the Organization of African Unity towards the realization of the solemn Declaration on the Denuclearization of Africa, in which the African Heads of State and Government announced their readiness to undertake, in an international treaty to be concluded under the auspices of the United Nations, not to manufacture or acquire control of nuclear weapons;

6. *Decides* to include in the provisional agenda of its thirty-first session the item entitled "Implementation of the Declaration on the Denuclearization of Africa."

2437th plenary meeting

Document No. XI

A Resolution of the United Nations General Assembly (31st Session, 10 December 1976)

Implementation of the Declaration on the Denuclearization of Africa

The General Assembly

Recalling its resolutions 1652 (XVI) of 24 November 1961, 2033 (XX) of 3 December 1965, 3261 E (XXIX) of 9 December 1974 and 3471 (XXX) of 11 December 1975, in which it called upon all States to consider and respect the continent of Africa, including the continental African States, Madagascar and other islands surrounding Africa, as a nuclear-weapon-free zone,

Recognizing that implementation of the Declaration on the Denuclearization of Africa adopted by the Assembly of Heads of State and Government of the Organization of African Unity in 1964 would contribute to the security of all the African States and to the goals of general and complete disarmament,

Bearing in mind that the Assembly of Heads of State and Government of the Organization of African Unity at its thirteenth ordinary session, held at Port Louis from 2 to 6 July 1976, expressed grave concern over the continuing collaboration between certain States Members of the United Nations and the racist régime of South Africa, particularly in the military and nuclear fields, thereby enabling it to acquire nuclear-weapon capability,

Concerned that further development of South Africa's military and nuclear-weapon potential would frustrate efforts to establish nuclear-weapon-free zones in Africa and elsewhere as an effective means for preventing the proliferation, both horizontal and vertical, of nuclear weapons and for contributing to the elimination of the danger of a nuclear holocaust,

1. *Reaffirms* its call upon all States to respect and abide by the Declaration on the Denuclearization of Africa;

2. *Further reaffirms* its call upon all States to consider and respect the continent of Africa, including the continental African

States, Madagascar and other islands surrounding Africa, as a nuclear-weapon-free zone;

3. *Appeals* to all States not to deliver to South Africa or place at its disposal any equipment or fissionable material or technology that will enable the racist régime of South Africa to acquire nuclear-weapon capability;

4. *Requests* the Secretary-General to render all necessary assistance to the Organization of African Unity towards the realization of its solemn Declaration on the Denuclearization of Africa, in which the African Heads of State and Government announced their readiness to undertake, in an international treaty to be concluded under the auspices of the United Nations, not to manufacture or acquire control of nuclear weapons;

5. *Decides* to include in the provisional agenda of its thirty-second session the item entitled "Implementation of the Declaration on the Denuclearization of Africa."

96th plenary meeting

Document No. XII

A Resolution of the United Nations General Assembly (36th Session, 9 December 1981)

Cessation of All Test Explosions of Nuclear Weapons

The General Assembly,

Bearing in mind that the complete cessation of nuclear-weapon tests , which has been examined for more than twenty-five years and on which the General Assembly has adopted more than forty resolutions, is a basic objective of the United Nations in the sphere of disarmament, to whose attainment it has repeatedly assigned the highest priority,

Stressing that on seven different occasions it has condemned such tests in the strongest terms and that, since 1974, it has stated its conviction that the continuance of nuclear-weapon testing will intensify the arms race, thus increasing the danger of nuclear war,

Reiterating the assertion made in several previous resolutions that, whatever may be the differences on the question of verification, there is no valid reason for delaying the conclusion of an agreement on a comprehensive test ban,

Recalling that since 1972 the Secretary-General has declared that all the technical and scientific aspects of the problem have been so fully explored tht only a political decision is now necessary in order to achieve final agreement, that when the existing means of verification are taken into account it is difficult to understand further delay in achieving agreement on an underground test ban, and that the potential risks of continuing underground nuclear-weapon tests would far outweigh any possible risks from ending such tests,

Recalling also that the Secretary-General, in his foreword to the report entitled "Comprehensive nuclear-test ban," reiterated with special emphasis the opinion he expressed nine years ago and, after specifically referring to it, added: "I still hold that belief. The problem can and should be solved now,"

Noting that in the same report, which was prepared in compliance with General Assembly decision 34/422 of 11 December

1979, the experts emphasized that non-nuclear-weapon States in general have come to regard the achievement of a comprehensive test ban as a litmus test of the determination of the nuclear-weapon States to halt the arms race, adding that verification of compliance no longer seems to be an obstacle to reaching agreement,

Taking into account that the three nuclear-weapon States which act as depositaries of the Treaty Banning Nuclear Weapon Tests in the Atmosphere, in Outer Space and under Water undertook in that Treaty, almost twenty years ago, to seek the achievement of the discontinuance of all test explosions of nuclear weapons for all time and that such an undertaking was explicitly reiterated in 1968 in the Treaty on the Non-Proliferation of Nuclear Weapons,

Recalling that in its resolution 35/145 A of 12 December 1980 it urged all States members of the Committee on Disarmament to support the establishment by the Committee, from the beginning of its session in 1981, of an *ad hoc* working group which should start the multilateral negotiations of a treaty for the prohibition of all nuclear-weapon tests,

Deploring that the Committee on Disarmament, as stated in paragraph 44 of its report to the Assembly, was prevented from responding to that exhortation owing to the negative attitude of two nuclear-weapon States,

1. *Reiterates once again its grave concern* that nuclear-weapon testing continues unabated against the wishes of the overwhelming majority of Member States;

2. *Reaffirms its conviction* that a treaty to achieve the prohibition of all nuclear-weapon-test explosions by all States for all time is a matter of the highest priority and constitutes a vital element for the success of efforts to prevent both vertical and horizontal proliferation of nuclear weapons and a contribution to nuclear disarmament;

3. *Urges* all States that have not yet done so to adhere without further delay to the Treaty Banning Nuclear Weapon Tests in the Atmosphere, in Outer Space and under Water and, meanwhile, to refrain from testing in the environments covered by that Treaty;

4. *Urges likewise* all States members of the Committee on Disarmament:

(*a*) To bear in mind that the consensus rule should not be used in such a manner as to prevent the establishment of subsidiary bodies for the effective discharge of the functions of the Committee;

Document No. XII

(b) To support the establishment by the Committee, from the beginning of its session in 1982, of an *ad hoc* working group which should start the multilateral negotiations of a treaty for the prohibition of all nuclear-weapon tests;

(c) To exert their best endeavours in order that the Committee may transmit the multilaterally negotiated text of such a treaty to the General Assembly at its second special session devoted to disarmament, to be held from 7 June to 9 July 1982;

5. *Calls upon* the States depositaries of the Treaty Banning Nuclear Weapon Tests in the Atmosphere, in Outer Space and under Water and the Treaty on the Non-Proliferation of Nuclear Weapons, by virtue of their special responsibilities under those two treaties and as a provisional measure, to bring to a halt without delay all nuclear-test explosions, either through a trilaterally agreed moratorium or through three unilateral moratoria;

2. *Decides* to include in the provisional agenda of its thirty-seventh session the item entitled "Cessation of all test explosions of nuclear weapons."

91st plenary meeting

Document No. XIII

A Resolution of the United Nations General Assembly (36th Session, 9 December 1981)

Conclusion of an International Convention on the Strengthening of the Security of Non-Nuclear-Weapon States Against the Use or Threat of Use of Nuclear Weapons

The General Assembly,

Convinced of the need to take effective measures for the strengthening of the security of States and prompted by the desire shared by all nations to eliminate war and prevent nuclear conflagration,

Taking into account the principle of non-use of force or threat of force enshrined in the Charter of the United Nations and reaffirmed in a number of United Nations declarations and resolutions,

Noting with satisfaction the desire of States in various regions to prevent nuclear weapons from being introduced into their territories, including through the establishment of nuclear-weapon-free zones, on the basis of arrangements freely arrived at among the States of the region concerned, and being anxious to contribute to the attainment of this objective,

Considering that, until nuclear disarmament is achieved on a universal basis, it is imperative for the international community to develop effective measures to ensure the security of non-nuclear-weapon States against the use or threat of use of nuclear weapons from any quarter,

Recognizing that effective measures to assure non-nuclear weapon States against the use or threat of use of nuclear weapons can constitute a positive contribution to the prevention of the spread of nuclear weapons,

Mindful of the statements made and views expressed by various States on the strengthening of the security of non-nuclear-weapon States,

Concerned at the continuing escalation of the arms race, in particular the nuclear-arms race, and the increased danger of recourse to the use or threat of use of nuclear weapons,

Deeply concerned at the plans for further stationing of nuclear weapons on the territories of non-nuclear-weapon States that could directly affect the security of non-nuclear-weapon States,

Desirous of promoting the implementation of paragraph 59 of the Final Document of the Tenth Special Session of the General Assembly, the first special session devoted to disarmament, in which it urged the nuclear-weapon States to pursue efforts to conclude, as appropriate, effective arrangements to assure non-nuclear-weapon States against the use or threat of use of nuclear weapons,

Recalling its resolutions 33/72 of 14 December 1978, 34/84 and 34/85 of 11 December 1979, 35/154 and 35/155 of 12 December 1980 and the relevant provisions of its resolution 35/46 of 3 December 1980,

Noting the consideration by the Committee on Disarmament in 1981 of the item entitled "Effective international arrangements to assure non-nuclear-weapon States against the use or threat of use of nuclear weapons" and the setting up of an *Ad Hoc* Working Group to continue the negotiations on this item,

Recalling the drafts of an international convention submitted on that item to the Committee on Disarmament in 1979 and noting with satisfaction that the idea of concluding such a convention has received widespread international support,

Taking note of the report of the Committee on Disarmament, including the report of the *Ad Hoc* Working Group on Effective International Arrangements to Assure Non-Nuclear-Weapon States against the Use or Threat of Use of Nuclear Weapons,

Wishing to promote an early and successful completion of the negotiations on the elaboration of a convention on the strengthening of the security of non-nuclear-weapon States against the use or threat of use of nuclear weapons,

Noting further that the idea of interim arrangements as a first step towards the conclusion of such a convention has also been considered in the Committee on Disarmament, particularly in the form of a Security Council resolution on this subject, and recalling the recommendation made in that respect by the General Assembly in paragraph 6 of its resolution 35/154,

Mindful of the second special session devoted to disarmament, to be held from 7 June to 9 July 1982, at which the General Assembly will review the progress achieved in the field of Disarmament, including the implementation of paragraph 59 of the Final Document of the Tenth Special Session of the General Assembly,

1. *Welcomes* the conclusion of the Committee on Disarmament that there is continuing recognition of the urgent need to reach agreement on effective international arrangements to assure non-nuclear-weapon States against the use or thrreat of use of nuclear weapons;

2. *Notes with satisfaction* that in the Committee on Disarmament there is once again no objection, in principle, to the idea of an international convention on this subject;

3. *Requests* the Committee on disarmament to continue the negotiations on the question of strengthening the security guarantees of non-nuclear-weapon States during its session in 1982;

4. *Calls upon* all States participating in those negotiations to make efforts for the elaboration and conclusion of an international convention on this matter;

5. *Calls once again upon* all nuclear-weapon States to make solemn declarations, identical in substance, concerning the non-use of nuclear weapons against non-nuclear-weapon States having no such weapons on their territories, as a first step towards the conclusion of an international convention, and recommends that the Security Council should examine such declarations and, if they all meet the above-mentioned objective, should adopt an appropriate resolution approving them;

Decides to include in the provisional agenda of its thirty-seventh session the item entitled "Conclusion of an international convention on the strengthening of the security of non-nuclear-weapon States against the use or threat of use of nuclear weapons."

91st plenary meeting

Document No. XIV

Resolutions and Decisions Adopted by the United Nations General Assembly during Its Tenth Special Session 23 May-30 June 1978

Final Document of the Tenth Special Session of the General Assembly

The General Assembly,

Alarmed by the threat to the very survival of mankind posed by the existence of nuclear weapons and the continuing arms race, and recalling the devastation inflicted by all wars,

Convinced that disarmament and arms limitation, particularly in the nuclear field, are essential for the prevention of the danger of nuclear war and the strengthening of international peace and security and for the economic and social advancement of all peoples, thus facilitating the achievement of the new international economic order,

Having resolved to lay the foundations of an international disarmament strategy which, through co-ordinated and persevering efforts in which the United Nations should play a more effective role, aims at general and complete disarmament under effective international control,

Adopts the following Final Document of this special session of the General Assembly devoted to disarmament:

Introduction

1. The attainment of the objective of security, which is an inseparable element of peace, has always been one of the most profound aspirations of humanity. States have for a long time sought to maintain their security through the possession of arms. Admittedly, their survival has, in certain cases, effectively depended on whether they could count on appropriate means of defence. Yet the accumulation of weapons, particularly nuclear weapons, today constitutes much more a threat than a protection

for the future of mankind. The time has therefore come to put an end to this situation, to abandon the use of force in international relations and to seek security in disarmament, that is to say, through a gradual but effective process beginning with a reduction in the present level of armaments. The ending of the arms race and the achievement of real disarmament are tasks of primary importance and urgency. To meet this historic challenge is in the political and economic interests of all the nations and peoples of the world as well as in the interests of ensuring their genuine security and peaceful future.

2. Unless its avenues are closed, the continued arms race means a growing threat to international peace and security and even to the very survival of mankind. The nuclear and conventional arms build-up threatens to stall the efforts aimed at reaching the goals of development, to become an obstacle on the road of achieving the new international economic order and to hinder the solution of other vital problems facing mankind.

3. The dynamic development of détente, encompassing all spheres of international relations in all regions of the world, with the participation of all countries, would create conditions conducive to the efforts of States to end the arms race, which has engulfed the world, thus reducing the danger of war. Progress on détente and progress on disarmament mutually complement and strengthen each other.

4. The Disarmament Decade solemnly declared in 1969 by the United Nations is coming to an end. Unfortunately, the objectives established on that occasion by the General Assembly appear to be as far away today as they were then, or even further because the arms race is not diminishing but increasing and outstrips by far the efforts to curb it. While it is true that some limited agreements have been reached, "effective measures relating to the cessation of the nuclear arms race at an early date and to nuclear disarmament" continue to elude man's grasp. Yet the implementation of such measures is urgently required. There has not been any real progress either that might lead to the conclusion of a treaty on general and complete disarmament under effective international control. Furthermore, it has not been possible to free any amount, however modest, of the enormous resources, both material and human, which are wasted on the unproductive and spiralling arms race and which should be made available for the purpose of eco-

nomic and social development, especially since such a race "places a great burden on both the developing and the developed countries."

5. The Members of the United Nations are fully aware of the conviction of their peoples that the question of general and complete disarmament is of utmost importance and that peace, security and economic and social development are indivisible, and they have therefore recognized that the corresponding obligations and responsibilities are universal.

6. Thus a powerful current of opinion has gradually formed, leading to the convening of what will go down in the annals of the United Nations as the first special session of the General Assembly devoted entirely to disarmament.

7. The outcome of this special session, whose deliberations have to a large extent been facilitated by the five sessions of the Preparatory Committee which preceded it, is the present Final Document. This introduction serves as a preface to the document which comprises also the following three sections: a Declaration, a Programme of Action and recommendations concerning the international machinery for disarmament negotiations.

8. While the final objective of the efforts of all States should continue to be general and complete disarmament under effective international control, the immediate goal is that of the elimination of the danger of a nuclear war and the implementation of measures to halt and reverse the arms race and clear the path towards lasting peace. Negotiations on the entire range of those issues should be based on the strict observance of the purposes and principles enshrined in the Charter of the United Nations, with full recognition of the role of the United Nations in the field of disarmament and reflecting the vital interest of all the peoples of the world in this sphere. The aim of the Declaration is to review and assess the existing situation, outline the objectives and the priority tasks and set forth fundamental principles for disarmament negotiations.

9. For disarmament—the aims and purposes of which the Declaration proclaims—to become a reality, it was essential to agree on a series of specific disarmament measures, selected by common accord as those on which there is a consensus to the effect that their subsequent realization in the short term appears to be feasible. There is also a need to prepare through agreed procedures a com-

prehensive disarmament programme. That programme, passing through all the necessary stages, should lead to general and complete disarmament under effective international control. Procedures for watching over the fulfillment of the obligations thus assumed had also to be agreed upon. That is the purpose of the Programme of Action.

10. Although the decisive factor for achieving real measures of disarmament is the "political will" of States, especially of those possessing nuclear weapons, a significant role can also be played by the effective functioning of an appropriate international machinery designed to deal with the problems of disarmament in its various aspects. Consequently, it would be necessary that the two kinds of organs required to that end, the deliberative and the negotiating organs, have the appropriate organization and procedures that would be most conducive to obtaining constructive results. The last section of the Final Document, section IV, has been prepared with that end in view.

* * *

33. The establishment of nuclear-weapon-free zones on the basis of agreements or arrangements freely arrived at among the States of the zone concerned and the full compliance with those agreements or arrangements, thus ensuring that the zones are genuinely free from nuclear weapons, and respect for such zones by nuclear-weapon States constitute an important disarmament measure.

* * *

60. The establishment of nuclear-weapon-free zones on the basis of arrangements freely arrived at among the States of the region concerned constitutes an important disarmament measure.

61. The process of establishing such zones in different parts of the world should be encouraged with the ultimate objective of achieving a world entirely free of nuclear weapons. In the process of establishing such zones, the characteristics of each region should be taken into account. The States participating in such zones should undertake to comply fully with all the objectives, purposes and principles of the agreements or arrangements establishing the

zones, thus ensuring that they are genuinely free from nuclear weapons.

62. With respect to such zones, the nuclear-weapon States in turn are called upon to give undertakings, the modalities of which are to be negotiated with the competent authority of each zone, in particular:

(a) To respect strictly the status of the nuclear-weapon-free zone;

(b) To refrain from the use or threat of use of nuclear weapons against the States of the zone.

63. In the light of existing conditions, and without prejudice to other measures which may be considered in other regions, the following measures are especially desirable:

(a) Adoption by the States concerned of all relevant measures to ensure the full application of the Treaty for the Prohibition of Nuclear Weapons in Latin America (Treaty of Tlatelolco), taking into account the views expressed at the tenth special session on the adherence to it;

(b) Signature and ratification of the Additional Protocols of the Treaty for the Prohibition of Nuclear Weapons in Latin America (Treaty of Tlatelolco) by the States entitled to become parties to those instruments which have not yet done so;

(c) In Africa, where the Organization of African Unity has affirmed a decision for the denuclearization of the region, the Security Council of the United Nations shall take appropriate effective steps whenever necessary to prevent the frustration of this objective;

(d) The serious consideration of the practical and urgent steps, as described in the paragraphs above, required for the implementation of the proposal to establish a nuclear-weapon-free zone in the Middle East, in accordance with the relevant General Assembly resolutions, where all parties directly concerned have expressed their support for the concept and where the danger of nuclear-weapon proliferation exists. The establishment of a nuclear-weapon-free zone in the Middle East would greatly enhance international peace and security. Pending the establishment of such a zone in the region, States of the region should solemnly declare that they will refrain on a reciprocal basis from producing, acquiring or in any other way possessing nuclear weapons and nuclear explosive devices and from permitting the stationing of nuclear weapons on their territory by any third party, and agree to place all their nuclear activities under International Atomic Energy Agency safeguards. Consideration should be given to a Security Council role in advancing the establishment of a nuclear-weapon-free zone in the Middle East.

* * *

64. The establishment of zones of peace in various regions of the world under appropriate conditions, to be clearly defined and determined freely by the States concerned in the zone, taking into account the characteristics of the zone and the principles of the Charter of the United Nations, and in conformity with international law, can contribute to strengthening the security of States within such zones and to international peace and security as a whole. In this regard, the General Assembly notes the proposals for the establishment of zones of peace, *inter alia*, in:

(a) South-East Asia where States in the region have expressed interest in the establishment of such a zone, in conformity with their views;

(b) The Indian Ocean, taking into account the deliberations of the General Assembly and its relevant resolutions and the need to ensure the maintenance of peace and security in the region.

65. It is imperative, as an integral part of the effort to halt and reverse the arms race, to prevent the proliferation of nuclear weapons. The goal of nuclear non-proliferation is on the one hand to prevent the emergence of any additional nuclear-weapon States besides the existing five nuclear-weapon States, and on the other progressively to reduce and eventually eliminate nuclear weapons altogether. This involves obligations and responsibilities on the part of both nuclear-weapon States and non-nuclear-weapon States, the former undertaking to stop the nuclear arms race and to achieve nuclear disarmament by urgent application of the measures outlined in the relevant paragraphs of this Final Document, and all States undertaking to prevent the spread of nuclear weapons.

* * *

68. Non-proliferation measures should not jeopardize the full exercise of the inalienable rights of all States to apply and develop their programmes for the peaceful uses of nuclear energy for economic and social development in conformity with their priorities, interests and needs. All States should also have access to and be free to acquire technology, equipment and materials for peaceful uses of nuclear energy, taking into account the particular needs of the developing countries. International co-operation in this field should be under agreed and appropriate international safeguards applied through the International Atomic Energy Agency on a non-discriminatory basis in order to prevent effectively the proliferation of nuclear weapons.

69. Each country's choices and decisions in the field of the peaceful uses of nuclear energy should be respected without jeopardizing their respective fuel cycle policies or international co-operation, agreements and contracts for the peaceful uses of nuclear energy, provided that the agreed safeguard measures mentioned above are applied.

70. In accordance with the principles and provisions of General Assembly resolution 32/50 of 8 December 1977, international co-operation for the promotion of the transfer and utilization of nuclear technology for economic and social development, especially in the developing countries, should be strengthened.

71. Efforts should be made to conclude the work of the International Nuclear Fuel Cycle Evaluation strictly in accordance with the objectives set out in the final communiqué of its Organizing Conference.

* * *

76. A convention should be concluded prohibiting the development, production, stockpiling and use of radiological weapons.

* * *

91. In order to facilitate the conclusion and effective implementation of disarmament agreements and to create confidence, States should accept appropriate provisions for verification in such agreements.

92. In the context of international disarmament negotiations, the problem of verification should be further examined and adequate methods and procedures in this field be considered. Every effort should be made to develop appropriate methods and procedures which are non-discriminatory and which do not unduly interfere with the internal affairs of other States or jeopardize their economic and social development.

93. In order to facilitate the process of disarmament, it is necessary to take measures and pursue policies to strengthen international peace and security and to build confidence among States. Commitment to confidence-building measures could significantly contribute to preparing for further progress in disarmament....

27th plenary meeting

SELECTED BIBLIOGRAPHY

A'ah, Hasan. "Egypt, Israel and the Nuclear Bomb" (in Arabic). *Al-Tali'ah* (Egypt), September, 1975.

Al-'Abid, Ibrahim. *Madkhal Ila al-Istratijiyah al-Isra'iliyah*. Beirut: Markaz al-Abhath, Munazzamat al-Tahrir al-Filastiniyah, 1971.

Ahmad, H. B. "The Development of Israel's Nuclear Capability" (in Arabic). *Al-Siyasah al-Dawliyah*, Vol. 17, No. 66, October 1981.

Allon, Yigal. *The Making of Israel's Army*. London: Vallentine Mitchell, 1970.

Amirie, Abbas, ed. *The Persian Gulf and Indian Ocean in International Politics*. Tehran: Institute for International Political Studies, 1975.

Aron, Raymond. *The Great Debate: Theories of Nuclear Strategy*. Garden City, New York: Doubleday, 1965.

Aronson, Shlomo. "Israel's Nuclear Options." ACIS Working Paper No. 17. Los Angeles: Center for Arms Control and International Security, University of California. November 1977.

———. "Nuclearization of the Middle East: A Dovish View." *Jerusalem Quarterly*, No. 2, Winter 1977.

———. "The Nuclear Factor in the Middle East (A) The Bomb in the Basement" (in Hebrew). *Ha'aretz*, November 14, 1980.

———. "The Nuclear Factor in the Middle East (B) The Nasirite Reply" (in Hebrew). *Ha'aretz*, November 16, 1980.

———. "The Nuclear Factor in the Middle East (C) Only As Far As the Green Line" (in Hebrew). *Ha'aretz*, November 18, 1980.

"The Atom Bomb in Israel: A Symposium." *New Outlook*, March-April 1961.

Al-'Askariyah al-Sahyuniyah, al-Mujallad al-Awwal: Al-Mu'assasah al-'Askariyah al-Israi'liyah: al-Nash'ah, al-Tatawwur, 1887-1977. Al-Qahirah: Markaz al-Dirasat al-Siyasiyah wa-al-Istratijiyah, Mu'assasat al-Ahram, 1972.

Aveneri, Uri. "The Balance of Terror" (in Hebrew). *Ha'olam Hazeh*, July 9, 1980.

Al-Ayyubi, Haytham. "The Truth About the Nuclear Challenge Between Egypt and Israel" (in Arabic). *Al-Usbu' al-'Arabi* (London), July 1 and July 8, 1974.

'Azmi, M. "Israel's Nuclear Option: A Strategic Necessity" (in Arabic). *Shu'un Filastiniyah*, No. 43, March 1975.

Bader, William B. *The United States and the Spread of Nuclear Weapons*. New York: Pegasus, 1968.

Baker, Steven J. "The Great Powers' Nonproliferation Policies Toward the Third World" in Milton Lutenberg, ed., *Great Power Intervention in the Middle East*. New York: Pergamon, 1979.

Barnaby, C. F., ed. *Preventing the Spread of Nuclear Weapons*. Pugwash Monograph 1. London: Souvenir Press, 1969.

Bar-Zohar, Michael. *Ben Gurion*. London: Weidenfeld and Nicolson, 1978.

Beaton, Leonard. *Must the Bomb Spread*? Harmondsworth: Penguin Books, 1966.

———. "Why Israel Does Not Need the Bomb." *New Middle East* (London), April 1969.

——— and Maddox, John. *The Spread of Nuclear Weapons*. London: Chatto & Windus for The Institute for Strategic Studies, 1962.

Becker, Bonita I. *Nuclear Israel: Potential and Policy*. M.A. Thesis. George Washington University, Department of Political Science, 1976.

Beckett, Brian. "Israel's Nuclear Options." *Middle East International*, No. 65, November 1976.

Beecher, William. "Israeli Missile Activity Stirs Conjecture on Atom Weapons." *International Herald Tribune*, October 6, 1971.

Bell, J. Bowyer. "Israel's Nuclear Option." *The Middle East Journal*, Vol. 26, No. 4, Autumn 1972.

Ben-Tzur, Avraham. "The Arabs and the Israeli Reactor." *New Outlook*, Vol. 4, No. 5, March-April 1961.

Benziman, 'Uzi. "When Sharon Says 'A Qualitative Gap,' What He Means?" (in Hebrew). *Ha'aretz*, February 22, 1982.

Beres, Louis Rene. "Terrorism and the Nuclear Threat in the Middle East." *Current History*, Vol. 70, NO. 412, January 1976.

———. "The Threat of Palestinian Nuclear Terrorism in the Middle East." *International Problems* (Tel Aviv), 15, Fall 1976.

Betts, Richard K. "Incentives for Nuclear Weapons: India, Pakistan, Iran." *Asian Survey*, November 1979.

Binder, David. "Israel and the Bomb." *Middle East International*, May 1976.

Burnham, David. "The Case of the Missing Uranium." *The Atlantic*, 243, April 1979.

Burns, Richard. *Salt, Nonproliferation and Nuclear Weapons—Free Zones: An Introduction*. Occasional Paper No. 6. Los Angeles: California State University Center for the Study of Armament and Disarmament, 1979.

Chari, P. "The Israeli Nuclear Option: Living Dangerously." *International Studies*, Vol. 16, No. 3, July-September 1977.

Committee for Nuclear Disarmament of the Arab-Israeli Region. "Keep Nuclear Weapons Out of Our Region." *New Outlook*, 9, July-August 1966.

Conference on Nuclear-Weapon-Free Zones, Nuclear Weapon-Free Zones: Vantage Conference Report, Airlie House, Warrenton, Virginia, October 7-9, 1975. Muscatine, Iowa: Stanley Foundation, 1975.

Cooper, Chester L. "Nuclear Hostages." *Foreign Policy*, Vol. 32, Fall 1978.

Crosbie, Sylvia. *A Tacit Alliance: France and Israel from Suez to the Six-Day War*. Princeton, 1974.

Dagan, D. "Israel As a 'Crazy State' " (in Hebrew). *Ha'aretz*, June 14, 1981.

Dowty, Alan. "Israel's Nuclear Policy" (in Hebrew). *Medinah, Mimshal Veyahasim Benle'umiim*, No. 7, Spring 1975.

———. "Israel and Nuclear Weapons." *Midstream*, 22, November 1976.

———. "Nuclear Proliferation: The Israeli Case." *International Studies Quarterly*, Vol. 22, No. 1, March 1978.

Dror, Y. "Small Powers Nuclear Policy: Research Methodology and Exploratory Analysis." *Jerusalem Journal of International Relations*, 1, 1975.
Dunn, Lewis A. "India, Pakistan, Iran... : A Nuclear Proliferation Chain?" in Overholt, William H. *Asia's Nuclear Future*. Boulder, Colorado: Westview Press, 1977.
Epstein, William. "Nuclear Proliferation in the Third World." *Journal of International Affairs (New York)*, 29, Fall 1975.
Evron, Yair. "A Nuclear Balance of Deterrence in the Middle East." *New Outlook*, Vol. 18, No. 5 (158), July-August 1975.
———. *Deterrence in the Middle East*. Forthcoming.
———. "Israel and the Atom: The Uses and Misuses of Ambiguity, 1957-1967." *ORBIS*, Vol. 17, No. 4, Winter 1974.
———. "Letter to the Editor." *Commentary*, February 1976.
———. "Some Effects of the Introduction of Nuclear Weapons in the Middle East" in Asher Arian, ed. *Israel: A Developing Society*. Tel Aviv: Pinhas Sapir Center for Development, Tel Aviv University, 1980.
———. "The Arab Position in the Nuclear Field: A Study of Policies Up to 1967." *Cooperation and Conflict* (Oslo), Vol. 8, No. 1, 1973.
———. *The Role of Arms Control in the Middle East*. London: The International Institute for Strategic Studies, 1977. Adelphi Papers, No. 138.
Falk, Richard A. "How a Nuclear War Can Start... in the Middle East." *Bulletin of the Atomic Scientists*, 35, April 1979.
———. *Nuclear Policy and World Order: Why Denuclearization*. New York: Institute for World Order, 1979.
Feldman, Shai. "A Nuclear Middle East." *Survival*, Vol. 23, No. 3, 1981.
———. "Peacemaking in the Middle East: The Next Step." *Foreign Affairs*, 59, No. 5, Spring 1981.
———. "The Raid on Osiraq: A Preliminary Assessment." CSS Memorandum, No. 5. Tel Aviv: Tel Aviv University Center for Strategic Studies, 1981.
Flapan, Simha. "Israel's Attitude Towards the NPT" in SIPRI. *Nuclear Proliferation Problems*. Stockholm, 1974.
———. "Nuclear Power in the Middle East." *New Outlook*, Vol. 17, No. 6 (152), July 1974.
———. "Nuclear Power in the Middle East." *New Outlook*, Vol. 17, No. 8, October 1974.
Freedman, Lawrence. "A Nuclear Middle East?" *Present Tense* (New York), Winter 1975.
———. "Israel's Nuclear Policy." *Survival*, Vol. 17, No. 3, May-June 1975.
Friedman, Todd. "Israel's Nuclear Option." *Bulletin of the Atomic Scientists*, Vol. 30, No. 7, September 1974.
Fukuyama, F. "Nuclear Shadowboxing: Soviet Intervention in the Middle East." *ORBIS*, Vol. 25, No. 3, 1981.
Gallois, Pierre M. *Balance of Terror: Strategy for the Nuclear Age*. Boston: Houghton Mifflin, 1961.
Gillette, Robert. "Uranium Enrichment: Rumors of Israeli Progress with Lasers." *Science* (Washington, D.C.), 183, March 22, 1974.

Goddmann, N. "The Future of Israel." *Foreign Affairs*, 48:3, April 1970.
Gottleib, Gideon. "Israel and the A-Bomb." *Commentary*, No. 31, February 1961.
Guhin, Michael A. *Nuclear Paradox: Security Risks of the Peaceful Atom*. Washington, D.C.: American Enterprise Institute for Public Policy Research, 1976.
Gupta, Sisir. "The Indian Dilemma" in Alastair Buchan, ed. *A World of Nuclear Powers?* Englewood Cliffs, N.J.: Prentice-Hall, 1966.
Haig, Alexander. "Department Statements on Israel's Raid on Iraq's Nuclear Facility." *Department of State Bulletin*, Vol. 81, No. 2053, August 1981.
Harkabi, Yehoshafat. *Milhamah Gar'init Veshalom Gar'ini* (in Hebrew). Tel Aviv: Ma'arakhot, 1964.
Harkavy, Robert E. *Spectre of a Middle Eastern Holocaust: The Strategic and Diplomatic Implications of the Israeli Nuclear Weapons Program*. Denver, Colorado: University of Denver Graduate School of International Studies, 1977. Monograph Series in World Affairs, Vol. 15, No. 4.
Harris, Leonard. *The Massada Plan*. New York: Crown, 1976.
Haselkorn, Avigdor. "Israel: From an Option to a Bomb in the Basement" in Robert M. Lawrence and Joel Larus, eds. *Nuclear Proliferation—Phase II*. Lawrence, Kansas: The University Press of Kansas, 1974.
Al-Hashimi, Sirin. "Israel's Nuclear Weapons" (in Arabic). *Majallat Markaz al-Dirasat al-Filastiniyah*, No. 27, March-April 1978.
Heikal, M. H. "Atomic Danger on the Middle East Horizon." *New Outlook*, September 1965.
———. "Frankly Speaking: The Israeli Atomic Bombs... Why Was Israel Obliged to Make the Bomb?" *Al-Ra'y* (Jordan), January 20, 22, 24, 26, 1976. Translated by Joint Publications Research Service, JPRS 66788, February 13, 1976.
———. "Israeli Nuclear Weapons, Supply of Arms from the West and the Question: Why Are the Arabs Silent?" (in Arabic). *Al-Anwar* (Lebanon), June 12, 1977.
———. "The Bomb" (in Arabic). *Al-Ahram* (Egypt), November 23, 1973.
———. *The Road to Ramadan*. New York: Quadrangle Press, 1975.
Hodes, Aubrey. "Implications of Israel's Nuclear Capability." *The Wiener Library Bulletin* (London), 22, Autumn, 1968.
Hoffmann, Stanley. "A New Policy for Israel." *Foreign Affairs*, 53, April 1975.
"Israel Has and Has Had the Bomb." *Middle East Perspectives*, Vol. 14, No. 4, July 1981.
"The Israeli Nuclear Option and the Raid on the Iraqi Reactor" (in Arabic). *Al-Ard*, Vol. 8, No. 24, September 7, 1981.
"Israel's Nuclear Weapons." *The Middle East*, No. 20, June 1976.
Jabber, Faud. *Israel and Nuclear Weapons: Present Option and Future Strategies*. London: Chatto & Windus for The International Institute for Strategic Studies, 1971.

Selected Bibliography

———. "Israel's Nuclear Option and U.S. Arms Control Policies." California Seminar on Arms Control and Foreign Policy. Research Paper, No. 9. Los Angeles: Crescent Publications, 1972.
———. "Israel's Nuclear Otions." *Journal of Palestine Studies*, Autumn 1971.
Jabber, Paul. "A Nuclear Middle East Infrastructure, Likely Military Postures and Prospects for Strategic Stability." ACIS Working Paper, No. 6. Los Angeles: Center for Arms Control and International Security, University of California, 1978.
Jaisjankar, S. "The Israeli Nuclear Option." *India Quarterly*, Vol. 34, No. 1, January-March 1978.
Jenkins, Brian Michael. "The Consequences of Nuclear Terrorism" in John Kerry King, ed. *International Political Effects of the Spread of Nuclear Weapons*. Washington, D.C.: GPO, 1979.
———. "The Impact of Nuclear Terrorism." Unpublished Paper, September 1978.
———. "The Potential for Nuclear Terrorism." Rand Memo P-5876. Santa Monica, California: Rand Corporation, May 1977.
Jones, R. "Nuclear Proliferation: Islam, the Bomb, and South Asia." *Washington Papers*, Vol. 9, No. 81, 1981.
Kemp, Geoffrey. "A Nuclear Middle East" in John Kerry King, ed. *International Political Effects of the Spread of Nuclear Weapons*. Washington, D.C.: GPO, 1979.
———. "Arms Traffic and Third-World Countries." *International Conciliation*. Carnegie Endowment for International Peace. March 1970.
———. "The New Strategic Map." *Survival*, Vol. 19, No. 2, March-April 1977.
Khalidi, Ahmad S. "An Appraisal of the Arab-Israeli Military Balance." *Middle East Forum*, XLII (3), 1966.
Kordova, Yishai and Avi-Shai. "The Soviet Nuclear Threat Toward the End of the Yom Kippur War" (in Hebrew). *Ma'arakhot* (Tel Aviv), No. 266, November 1978.
Krieger, David. "What Happens If . . . ? Terrorists, Revolutionaries, and Nuclear Weapons" in Joseph I. Coffey, ed. *Nuclear Proliferation: Prospects, Problems, Proposals*. Annals of the American Academy of Political Science (Philadelphia), No. 430, March 1977.
LeFever, Ernest. *Nuclear Arms in the Third World*. Washington, D.C.: Brookings Institution, 1979.
Livneh, Eliezer. "Israel Must Come Out for Denuclearization." *New Outlook*, 9, June 1966.
Manning, Robert and Talbot, Stephen. "American Cover-Up on Israeli Bomb." *The Middle East*, No. 68, June 1980.
Marshall, Eliot. "Iraqi Nuclear Program Halted by Bombing." *Science*, October 31, 1980.
Martin, B. "Iraq's Nuclear Weapons: A Prospectus." *Middle East Review*, Vol. 13, No. 2, 1980-81.

McPeak, Merrill A. "Israel: Borders and Security." *Foreign Affairs*, 54, April 1976.
Moss, Norman. *The Politics of Uranium*. New York: Universe, 1982.
Mruwwih, Yusuf. *Al-Abhath al-Dhariyah al-Isra'iliyah*. Beirut: Markaz al-Abhath, 1969.
———. *Akhtar al-Taqaddum al-'Ilmi fi Isra'il*. Beirut: Markaz al-Abhath, 1967.
Muslih, B. "Israel and the Proliferation of Nuclear Weapons" (in Arabic). *Majallat Markaz al-Dirasat al-Filastiniyah*, No. 29, July-August 1978.
Mustafa, A. "Arab Nuclear Potential" (in Arabic). *Al-Mustaqbal al-'Arabi*, No. 9, September 1979.
Al-Muwafi, A. "The Nuclear Arms Race in the Arab Region" (in Arabic). *Qadaya 'Arabiyah*, Vol. 8, No. 4, April 1981.
Al-Nasr, Muhammad Jabir. "The Arab Nuclear Program... When and Where?" (in Arabic). *Al-Anwar* (Lebanon), June 26, 1974.
Al-Nashif, Taysir. "The Israeli Military Thinking about the Military Conflict in the Middle East" (in Arabic). *Shu'un Filastiniyah*, No. 112, March 1981.
Nimrod, Yoram. "Atomic Weapons in Israel." *New Outlook*, Vol. 21, No.5, September 1978.
———. "Non-Nuclear Deterrence." *New Outlook*, Vol. 19, No. 3 (166), April-May 1976.
———. "Nuclear Uncertainty and Arab Reactions" (in Hebrew). *Davar*, December 2, 1980.
Norton, A. "Nuclear Terrorism and the Middle East." *Military Review*, Vol. 56, No. 4, April 1976.
"Nuclear Weapons in the Middle East." *Bulletin of the Peace Proposals*, No. 4, 1976.
Orfalea, G. "Nuclear Weapons and Israel." *Link*, Vol. 14, No. 4, September-October 1981.
Pajak, Roger F. *Nuclear Proliferation in the Middle East: Implications for the Superpowers*. Washington, D.C.: National Defense University Press, 1982.
Palestine Liberation Organization, Planning Center. "The Nuclear Option in the Middle East" (in Arabic). *Al-Fikr al-'Arabi al-Mu'asir*, Nos. 14-15, August-September, 1981.
Palit, D. K. and Namboodiri, P. K. S. *Pakistan's Islamic Bomb*. New Delhi: Vikas, 1979.
Peled, M. "An Adventure in Baghdad" (in Hebrew). *Ha'aretz*, June 11, 1981.
Peters, Rita Putins. *The Politics of Non-Aligned States and the Nuclear Test Ban Treaty*. Ann Arbor, Mich.: University Microfilms, 1973. Dissertation. Boston University, Department of Political Science.
Pranger, Robert J. "Nuclear War Comes to the Middle East' in Michael P. Hamilton. *To Avoid Catastrophe; a Study in Future Nuclear Weapons Policy*. Grand Rapids, Mich.: William B. Eerdmans, 1977.

Selected Bibliography

―――― and Tahtinen, Dale R. "Nuclear Legacy of the October 1973 Middle East War" in *International Symposium on the 1973 October War: Proceedings*. Cairo: Ministry of War, 1976.

――――. *Nuclear Threat in the Middle East*. Washington, D.C.: American Enterprise Institute for Public Policy Research, 1975.

"Prospects to Export Nuclear Technology to Egypt and Israel Discussed before House Subcommittees." *Department of State Bulletin*, Vol. 71, No. 1832, August 5, 1974.

Quester, George H. "Israel and the Nuclear Non-Proliferation Treaty." *Bulletin of the Atomic Scientists*, 25, June, 1969.

――――. *The Politics of Nuclear Proliferation*. London and Baltimore: Johns Hopkins University Press, 1974.

――――. "The Shah and the Bomb." *Political Science* (Wellington), 8, March 1977.

Al-Rawi, Jabir I. "The Zionist Aggression on the Iraqi Nuclear Installations and the Rule of International Law" (in Arabic) *Afaq 'Arabiyah*, Vol. 8, No. 3, November 1982.

Rosen, Steven J. "A Stable System of Mutual Nuclear Deterrence in the Arab-Israeli Conflict." *American Political Science Review*, 71, December 1977.

――――. "Nuclearization and Stability in the Middle East" in Onkar Marwah and Ann Schulz, eds. *Nuclear Proliferation and the Near-Nuclear Countries*. Cambridge, Mass.: Ballinger, 1975.

―――― and Indyk, M. "The Temptation to Pre-Empt in a Fifth Arab-Israeli War." *ORBIS*, Vol. 20, No. 2, 1976.

Rosenbaum, David M. "Nuclear Terror." *International Security*, 1 (3), Winter 1977.

Rutherford, E. "Israel and the Bomb." *Cambridge Review*, 2, December 1967.

Schiff, Ze'ev. "A Nuclear Bomb in the Middle East" (in Hebrew). *Ha'aretz*, June 27, 1980.

――――. "Begin's Doctrine" (in Hebrew). *Ha'aretz*, July 19, 1981.

Schweitzer, Avraham. "The Nuclear option's Importance." *SWASIA*, Vol. 3, No. 14, April 9, 1976.

Sisco, Joseph J. "Department [of State] Discusses Proposed Nuclear Reactor Agreements with Egypt and Israel." *Department of State Bulletin* (Washington, D.C.), 71, October 7, 1974.

Smith, Hedrick. "U.S. Assumes the Israelis Have A-Bomb or Its Parts." *The New York Times*, July 18, 1970.

Stockholm International Peace Research Institute. *The Near-Nuclear Countries and the N.P.T.* New York: Humanities Press, 1972.

Tahir-Kheli, Shirin. "Pakistan's Nuclear Option and U.S. Policy." *ORBIS*, Vol. 22, No. 2, 1978.

Tucker, Robert W. "Israel and the United States: From Dependence to Nuclear Weapons?" *Commentary*, Vol. 60, No. 5, November 1975.

United Nations, Centre for Disarmament. *Study on Israeli Nuclear Armament*. New York: United Nations, 1982.

United Nations, Conference of the Committee on Disarmament. *Comprehensive Study of the Question of Nuclear-Weapon-Free Zones in All Its Aspects*. New York: United Nations, 1976.

United States. *Senate Delegation Report on American Foreign Policy and Non-Proliferation Interests in the Middle East*. 95th Congress, 1st Session. Washington, D.C.: Government Printing Office, 1977.

United States, Congress, House, Committee on Foreign Affairs. Resolutions of Inquiry into Proposed Nuclear Agreements with Egypt and Israel: Hearings before the Committee on Foreign Affairs, House of Representatives, 93rd Congress, 2nd Session, on H. Res. 1189 and 1219. July 9, 1974. Washington: GPO, 1974.

"Ups and Downs in Israel Strategy Since 1967." *New Middle East*, 18, March 1970.

Valery, Nicholas. "Israel's Silent Gamble with the Bomb." *New Scientist*, December 12, 1974.

Van Creveld, M. "Israel and Nuclear Weapons." *The Wiener Library Bulletin*, Vol. 30, Nos. 41-42, 1977.

Von Clausewitz, Karl. *On War*. Book III. Translated by J. J. Graham (1908). Edited by Anatol Rapoport. Baltimore: Penguin Books, 1968.

Wade, Nicholas. "France, Iraq, and the Bomb." *Science*, August 29, 1980.

Waltzer, Michael. "The New Terrorists." *The New Republic*, August 30, 1975.

Weinbaum, M. G. and Sen Gautam. "Pakistan Enters the Middle East." *ORBIS*, Fall 1978.

Weissman, Steve and Herbert Krosney. *The Islamic Bomb*. New York: Times Books, 1981.

Whetten, L. L. "June 1967 to June 1971: Four Years of Canal War Reconsidered." *New Middle East*, June 1971.

Willrich, Mason. "Guarantees to Non-Nuclear Nations." *Foreign Affairs*, July 1966.

——— and Theodore Taylor. *Nuclear Theft: Risks and Safeguards*. Cambridge: Ballinger, 1974.

Windsor, P. "The Middle East and the World Balance." *World Today*, July 1967.

Wittman, George. "Intelligence Forecast: The Persian Gulf in a Nuclear Proliferated World" in Lewis Dunn, ed. *US Defense Planning for a More Proliferated World*. Croton-on-Hudson, N.Y.: Hudson Institute, 1979.

Yiftah, Shim'on. *Ha'idan Hagar'ini Bamizrah Hatikhon*. Tel Aviv: 'Am 'Oved, 1976.

Yisrael-'Arav: Himush o Peruz Atomi. Tel Aviv: 'Amikam, 1963.

Zoppo, Ciro E. "The Nuclear Genie in the Middle East." *New Outlook*, Vol. 18, No. 2 (157), February 1975.

INDEX

'Abd al-Nasir, J., 26
Arab reaction to Israeli nuclear activity, 25, 26, 44
'Arafat, Y., 67

Ben Gurion, D., 57
Bergmann, E. D., 19

Dayan, Moshe, 45
Denuclearization, 86, 87, 89, 98, 113, 114, 115, 116, 129
Dimona nuclear reactor, 16, 56, 57; plutonium production in, 17; under supervision of the Ministry of Defense, 18
Disarmament Decade, 126
Distances, 60, 62, 68, 72, 73, 75, 78
Dostrowsky, Israel, 15, 16

Egypt, foreign scientists in, 27; nuclear activity in, 26; relations of Western states with, in the nuclear field, 28, 29; uranium deposits in, 30

Gallois, Pierre, 48

Indian Ocean, 107, 108, 130
International Atomic Energy Agency (IAEA) safeguards, 91, 93, 102, 104, 106, 111, 112, 130, 131
Iraq, 106; nuclear installations in, 106, 112; nuclear relations between France and, 30-31
Israel: Assistance from the West to, 16, 17; capability to manufacture nuclear weapons, 20; CIA evidence on, manufacturing of nuclear weapons, 21-22; nuclear agreement between France and, 16; nuclear research in, 15; plutonium separation plants in, 19; United States nuclear cooperation with, 16, 17, 18, 111, 112

Israeli Atomic Energy Commission, 15
Israeli nuclear option: 'Abd al-Nasir and, 39; Arab modernization and, 40; as a function of a sense of insecurity, 37; changing international circumstances and, 38, 47; demographic and territorial size and, 40, 42; deterrence and, 43; economic difficulties and, 41; external danger and, 37; negotiated settlement with Arab states and, 43, 47; rising costs of conventional weapons and, 41; self-reliance and, 39; social background of political elites and, 39

Jabber, Fuad, 76

Military balance, 47, 74
Military gap, 46

Non-Proliferation Treaty (NPT), 32, 44, 56, 98, 101, 104, 106, 111, 118; Israel's attitude towards, 33; political settlement and, 58; safeguards, 33; Sh. Peres and, 57-58
Nuclear balance, 76, 80; arms race and, 69
Nuclear delivery: Diamant missile, 57; Jericho missile, 23, 78, 79
Nuclear deterrence, 49, 69, 72, 73, 75, 76; Allon on, 45; bluff and 55, 71; Evron on, 46; Flapan on, 46; Goldmann on, 46, 78; Haselkorn on, 45, 53; mentality and, 80; nuclear uncertainty and, 57; psychological balance and, 78; technology and, 77; values and, 67
Nuclear dispersion, 72, 79
Nuclear mobility, 72

141

Nuclear strike and confidence, 54, 71
Nuclear technology: Peaceful application, 91, 92, 93, 94, 113
Nuclear tests, 117, 118, 119; in Israel, 22, 23, 24, 25; verification of, 117, 118, 131, 132
Nuclear uncertainty, 55, 56, 69
Nuclear war in the Middle East: By accident, 68; character of leaders and, 80; interdiction and, 60; length of confrontation and, 64; losses in, 64; national survival and, 59-60; nuclear deterrence and, 63; Palestinian guerrillas and, 67; pre-emption and, 61-62; quantitative and qualitative changes and, 62-63; shift in Western policies and, 65; surprise and, 61; values and, 80; world public opinion and, 59
Nuclear-weapon-free zones, 111, 113, 115, 116, 121, 128, 129

Nuclear weapons: introduction into the Middle East, 23, 55-56, 79
October 1973 war, 48, 75
Outer space, 86, 92, 118, 119
Pakistan's nuclear relations with European firms, 31
Phosphate in Al-Naqab (Negev), 19
Population density, 79
Pre-emption: France, 48
Al-Qadhdhafi's interest in nuclear devices, 30
Qattarah Depression, 29
South Africa, 111, 115, 116
Soviet Union, 47, 48, 49, 61, 70, 71, 72, 75, 76, 77, 78
Treaty of Tlatelolco, 129
United Nations supervision, 50, 56
United States, 49, 70, 71, 72, 75, 76, 77, 78; pre-emption and, 48
Weizmann, Ch., 15
Zones of peace, 130